COLLECTED POEMS
Jane Kenyon

From Room to Room

Twenty Poems of Anna Akhmatova (Translations)

The Boat of Quiet Hours

Let Evening Come

Constance

Otherwise: New & Selected Poems

A Hundred White Daffodils (Essays, Interview, The Akhmatova Translations, Newspaper Columns, and One Poem)

Collected Poems

JANE KENYON

Graywolf Press

SAINT PAUL, MINNESOTA

Publication of this volume is made possible in part by a grant provided by the Minnesota State Arts Board, through an appropriation by the Minnesota State Legislature; a grant from the Wells Fargo Foundation Minnesota; and a grant from the National Endowment for the Arts, which believes that a great nation deserves great art. Significant support has also been provided by the Bush Foundation; Target; the McKnight Foundation; and other generous contributions from foundations, corporations, and individuals. To these organizations and individuals we offer our heartfelt thanks.

Published by Graywolf Press
2402 University Avenue, Suite 203
Saint Paul, Minnesota 55114
All rights reserved.

www.graywolfpress.org

Published in the United States of America

ISBN 978-1-55597-428-2 (cloth)
ISBN 978-1-55597-478-7 (paperback)

2 4 6 8 9 7 5 3 1

Library of Congress Control Number: 2007924766

Cover design: Christa Schoenbrodt, Studio Haus

Cover painting: Roloef Koets (1592–1655), Still-life (panel)
RAF81439, Rafael Valls Gallery, London, UK.
Reprinted by permission of The Bridgeman
Art Library International.

Acknowledgments

Grateful acknowledgment is made to the editors of the following in which the material listed below first appeared:

From Room to Room by Jane Kenyon, Alice James Books, 1978

The Boat of Quiet Hours by Jane Kenyon, Graywolf Press, 1986

Let Evening Come by Jane Kenyon, Graywolf Press, 1990

Constance by Jane Kenyon, Graywolf Press, 1993

Otherwise: New & Selected Poems by Jane Kenyon, Graywolf Press, 1996

A Hundred White Daffodils by Jane Kenyon, Graywolf Press, 1999

"What It's Like" first appeared in *Ploughshares,* Summer 1979.

"Indolence in Early Winter" first appeared in *New Letters,* Fall 1980, and was reprinted in *New Letters,* Spring/Summer 1983.

"Breakfast at the Mount Washington Hotel" first appeared in *The Iowa Review,* Spring/Summer 1986.

"At the IGA: Franklin, New Hampshire" first appeared in *Ontario Review,* Fall/Winter 1989.

Twenty Poems of Anna Akhmatova, translated from the Russian by Jane Kenyon with Vera Sandomirsky Dunham, Eighties Press/Ally Press, 1985

Contents

The Boat of Quiet Hours (1986)

Constance (1993)

Last Poems
in *Otherwise (1996)* and in *A Hundred White Daffodils (1999)*

Uncollected Poems

Translations:
Twenty Poems of Anna Akhmatova (1985)

From Room to Room
(1978)

— for my family

1

Under a Blue Mountain

For the Night

The mare kicks
in her darkening stall, knocks
over a bucket.

The goose . . .

The cow keeps a peaceful brain
behind her broad face.

Last light moves
through cracks in the wall,
over bales of hay.

And the bat lets
go of the rafter, falls
into black air.

Leaving Town

It was late August when we left. I gave away my plants, all but a few. The huge van, idling at the curb all morning, was suddenly gone.

We got into the car. Friends handed us the cats through half-closed windows. We backed out to the street, the trailer behind, dumb and stubborn.

We talked little, listening to a Tiger double-header on the car radio. Dust and cat hair floated in the light. I ate a cheese sandwich I didn't want.

During the second game, the signal faded until it was too faint to hear. I felt like a hand without an arm. We drove all night and part of the next morning.

From Room to Room

Here in this house, among photographs
of your ancestors, their hymnbooks and old
shoes . . .

       I move from room to room,
a little dazed, like the fly. I watch it
bump against each window.

I am clumsy here, thrusting
slabs of maple into the stove.
Out of my body for a while,
weightless in space. . . .

            Sometimes
the wind against the clapboard
sounds like a car driving up to the house.

My people are not here, my mother
and father, my brother. I talk
to the cats about weather.

"Blessed be the tie that binds . . ."
we sing in the church down the road.
And how does it go from there? The tie . . .

the tether, the hose carrying
oxygen to the astronaut,
turning, turning outside the hatch,
taking a look around.

Here

You always belonged here.
You were theirs, certain as a rock.
I'm the one who worries
if I fit in with the furniture
and the landscape.

         But I "follow too much
the devices and desires of my own heart."

Already the curves in the road
are familiar to me, and the mountain
in all kinds of light,
treating all people the same.
And when I come over the hill,
I see the house, with its generous
and firm proportions, smoke
rising gaily from the chimney.

I feel my life start up again,
like a cutting when it grows
the first pale and tentative
root hair in a glass of water.

Two Days Alone

You are not here. I keep
the fire going, though it isn't cold,
feeding the stove-animal.
I read the evening paper
with five generations
looking over my shoulder.

In the woodshed
darkness is all around and inside me.
The only sound I hear
is my own breathing. Maybe
I don't belong here.
Nothing tells me that I don't.

The Cold

I don't know why it made me happy to see the pond ice over in a day, turning first hazy, then white. Or why I was glad when the thermometer read twenty-four below, and I came back to bed—the pillows cold, as if I had not been there two minutes before.

This Morning

The barn bears the weight
of the first heavy snow
without complaint.

White breath of cows
rises in the tie-up, a man
wearing a frayed winter jacket
reaches for his milking stool
in the dark.

The cows have gone into the ground,
and the man,
his wife beside him now.

A nuthatch drops
to the ground, feeding
on sunflower seed and bits of bread
I scattered on the snow.

The cats doze near the stove.
They lift their heads
as the plow goes down the road,
making the house
tremble as it passes.

The Thimble

I found a silver thimble
on the humusy floor of the woodshed,
neither large nor small, the open end
bent oval by the wood's weight,
or because the woman who wore it
shaped it to fit her finger.

Its decorative border of leaves, graceful
and regular, like the edge of acanthus
on the tin ceiling at church . . .
repeating itself over our heads
while we speak in unison
words the wearer must have spoken.

Changes

The cast-iron kitchen range
grows rust like fur
in the cold barn. Oh,
we still keep animals—cats—
inside the house, while
the last load of hay
turns dusty on the barn floor.

Gazing at us from parlor walls,
the gallery of ancestors
must think we're *foolish,*
like Charlie Dolbey,
who used to chase cars
and bicycles, howling,
waving his arms in the air.

Finding a Long Gray Hair

I scrub the long floorboards
in the kitchen, repeating
the motions of other women
who have lived in this house.
And when I find a long gray hair
floating in the pail,
I feel my life added to theirs.

Hanging Pictures in Nanny's Room

When people reminisce about her they say how cross she was. I saw a photograph of her down in the parlor, her jaw like a piece of granite. You'd have to plow around it.

But look at this: huge garlands of pink roses on the sunny walls. A border near the ceiling undulates like the dancers' arms in Matisse's painting.

I put up a poster of Mary Cassatt's "Woman Bathing." No doubt Nanny bent here summer mornings, her dress down about her waist, water dripping through her fingers into the china bowl.

In the drawer of the dresser I found a mouse nest, with its small hoard of seeds. But also I found a pincushion, many-colored squares of silk sewn together and then embroidered. Nanny taught the girls in the family how to do fancywork. And if the stitches weren't good enough, you had to take them out and start over.

And if people weren't good enough, if your husband who worked on the railroad was a philanderer, well, you could move back to the house where you were born. You could go up to your room and rock awhile, or read from the Scriptures, or snip from the newspaper the latest episode of *Pollyanna: Or, The Glad Book.*

You pasted the clippings into an outdated Report on Agriculture, a big book, well bound. The story could go on for a long time. . . .

And when your sister's girls came upstairs to visit their fierce aunt, you would read aloud: "Miss Polly Harrington entered her kitchen hurriedly this June morning. Miss Polly did not usually make hurried movements; she specially prided herself on her repose of manner . . ."

In Several Colors

Every morning, cup of coffee
in hand, I look out at the mountain.
Ordinarily, it's blue, but today
it's the color of an eggplant.

And the sky turns
from gray to pale apricot
as the sun rolls up
Main Street in Andover.

I study the cat's face
and find a trace of white
around each eye, as if
he made himself up today
for a part in the opera.

The Clothes Pin

How much better it is
to carry wood to the fire
than to moan about your life.
How much better
to throw the garbage
onto the compost, or to pin the clean
sheet on the line
with a gray-brown wooden clothes pin!

2

Edges of the Map

~

The Needle

Grandmother, you are as pale
as Christ's hands on the wall above you.
When you close your eyes you are all
white—hair, skin, gown. I blink
to find you again in the bed.

I remember once you told me
you weighed a hundred and twenty-three,
the day you married Grandfather.
You had handsome legs. He watched you
working at the sink.

The soft ring is loose on your hand.
I hated coming here.
I know you can't understand me.
I'll try again,
like the young nurse with the needle.

My Mother

My mother comes back from a trip downtown to the dime store. She has brought me a surprise. It is still in her purse.

She is wearing her red shoes with straps across the in-step. They fasten with small white buttons, like the eyes of fish.

She brings back zippers and spools of thread, yellow and green, for her work, which always takes her far away, even though she works upstairs, in the room next to mine.

She is wearing her blue plaid full-skirted dress with the large collar, her hair fastened up off her neck. She looks pretty. She always dresses up when she goes downtown.

Now she opens her straw purse, which looks like a small suitcase. She hands me the new toy: a wooden paddle with a red rubber ball attached to it by an elastic string. Sometimes when she goes downtown, I think she will not come back.

Cleaning the Closet

This must be the suit you wore
to your father's funeral:
the jacket
dusty, after nine years,
and hanger marks on the shoulders,
sloping like the lines
on a woman's stomach, after
having a baby, or like the down-
turned corners
of your mouth, as you watch me
fumble to put the suit
back where it was.

Ironing Grandmother's Tablecloth

As a bride, you made it smooth,
pulling the edges straight, the corners square.
For years you went over the same piece
of cloth, the way Grandfather walked to work.

This morning I move the iron across the damask,
back and forth, up and down. You are ninety-four.
Each day you dress yourself, then go back to bed
and listen to radio sermons, staring at the ceiling.

When I visit, you tell me your troubles:
how my father left poisoned grapefruit on the back
porch at Christmas, how somebody comes at night
to throw stones at the house.

The streets of your brain become smaller,
old houses torn down. Talking to me
is hard work, keeping things straight,
whose child I am, whether I have children.

The Box of Beads

This morning I came across
a box of my grandmother's beads,
all tangled, and coming unstrung.

I hardly knew my mother's parents.
They lived in California—the edge of the map—
when I was growing up.

Grandfather fastened this necklace
while she held her hair.
Looking at him in the dressing-table mirror,
she let her hair
fall on the backs of his hands.

What do I know about her?
She loved to have company for dinner.
She sang contralto in the choir.
When they lived in Winnetka,
before my mother was born,
she used to put on a hat, take the train
into Chicago, and have coconut pie
at Marshall Field's.

I went to visit when I was seven,
a long train ride across the country.
One day she took me to the Farmer's Market
in Los Angeles. She bought me
a beaded belt that said "California,"
and a Mexican jumping bean in a plastic box.
She wore perfume.
She had a kumquat tree in her garden.

When she died, cousins sent me
her Turkish coffeepot, and my mother
gave me this box of beads.
Here is an apricot-colored glass
pendant. Some long, opaque
black beads . . . some green ones, small and bright
as fresh peas. Here is the clasp
that held them around her neck.

3

Colors

At a Motel near O'Hare Airport

I sit by the window all morning
watching the planes make final approaches.
Each of them gathers and steadies itself
like a horse clearing a jump.

I look up to see them pass,
so close I can see the rivets
on their bellies, and under their wings,
and at first I feel ashamed,
as if I had looked up a woman's skirt.

How beautiful that one is,
slim-bodied and delicate
as a fox, poised and intent
on stealing a chicken
from a farmyard.

And now a larger one, its
tail shaped like a whale's.
They call it sounding
when a whale dives,
and the tail comes out of the water
and flashes in the light
before going under.

Here comes a 747,
slower than the rest,
phenomenal, like some huge
basketball player
clearing space for himself
under the basket.

How wonderful to be that big
and to fly through the air,
and to make such a big shadow
in the parking lot of a motel.

The First Eight Days of the Beard

1. A page of exclamation points.
2. A class of cadets at attention.
3. A school of eels.
4. Standing commuters.
5. A bed of nails for the swami.
6. Flagpoles of unknown countries.
7. Centipedes resting on their laurels.
8. The toenails of the face.

Changing Light

Clouds move over the mountain,
methodical as ancient
scholars.
        Sun comes out
in the high pasture where
cows feel heat
between their shoulder blades.

The Socks

While you were away
I matched your socks
and rolled them into balls.
Then I filled your drawer with
tight dark fists.

The Shirt

The shirt touches his neck
and smooths over his back.
It slides down his sides.
It even goes down below his belt—
down into his pants.
Lucky shirt.

Starting Therapy

1

The psychiatrist moves toward me,
a child's sweater in his hands.
It's my old white cardigan.
He's going to make me wear it.
He puts my arm into one of the sleeves.
He puts it on me backwards.
This thing is a straightjacket!
Anybody in his right mind can see
this sweater doesn't fit.

2

Thinking someone is at the door
I open it to find a small brain
hovering over the porch.
It won't come in and it won't go away.
I let the screen door slam.
It sounds like the door to the apartment
where I used to live.
No, it's the door to my parents' house
where we lived when I was four.

Colors

(for S.D.)

Sometimes I agreed with you
to make you stop telling me things.
I was a fist closed around a rock.

For a long time nothing changed.
It was like driving all day through Texas.

But now I've stopped
tearing the arm off the waiting-room chair,
and sneaking back at night to fix it.

And the change was like light
moving through a prism, red
turning to yellow, green to blue,
and all by insensible degrees.

From the Back Steps

A bird begins to sing,
hesitates, like a carpenter
pausing to straighten a nail, then
begins again.
The cat lolls in the shade
under the parked car, his head
in the wheel's path.
I bury the thing I love.

But the cat continues to lie
comfortably, right where he is,
and no one will move the car.
My own violence falls away
like paint peeling from a wall.
I am choosing a new color
to paint my house, though I'm still
not sure what the color will be.

Cages

1

Driving to Winter Park in March,
past Cypress Gardens and the baseball camps,
past the dead beagle in the road, his legs
outstretched, as if he meant to walk
on his side in the next life.

At night, the air
smells like a cup of jasmine tea.
The night-bloomer, white
flowering jasmine,
and groves of orange trees
breathing through their sweet skins.

And cattle in the back
of the truck, staggering
as the driver turns off the highway.

2

By the pool, here at the hotel,
animals in cages to amuse us:
monkeys, peacocks, a pair of black swans,
rabbits, parrots, cockatoos,
flamingoes holding themselves on one leg,
perfectly still, as if they loathed
touching the ground.

The black swan floats
in three inches of foul water,
its bright bill thrust under its wing.

And the monkeys: one of them
reaches through the cage
and grabs for my pen, as if
he had finally decided to write a letter
long overdue.

And one lies in the lap of another.
They look like Mary and Jesus
in the Pietà, one searching for fleas
or lice on the other, for succour
on the body of the other—
some particle of comfort, some
consolation for being in this life.

3

And the body, what about the body?
Sometimes it is my favorite child,
uncivilized as those spider monkeys
loose in the trees overhead.

They leap, and cling with their strong
tails, they steal food
from the cages—little bandits.
If Chaucer could see them,
he would change "lecherous as a sparrow"
to "lecherous as a monkey."

And sometimes my body disgusts me.
Filling and emptying it disgusts me.
And when I feel that way

I treat it like a goose with its legs
tied together, stuffing it
until the liver is fat enough
to make a tin of paté.
Then I have to agree that the body
is a cloud before the soul's eye.

This long struggle to be at home
in the body, this difficult friendship.

4

People come here when they are old
for slow walks on the beach
with new companions. Mortuaries
advertise on bus-stop benches.
At night in nearby groves,
unfamiliar constellations
rise in a leafy sky,
and in the parks, mass plantings
of cannas are blooming
their outrageous blooms,
as if speaking final thoughts,
no longer caring what anyone thinks. . . .

4

Afternoon in the House

At the Feeder

First the Chickadees take
their share, then fly
to the bittersweet vine,
where they crack open the seeds,
excited, like poets
opening the day's mail.

And the Evening Grosbeaks—
those large and prosperous
finches—resemble skiers
with the latest equipment, bright
yellow goggles on their faces.

Now the Bluejay comes in
for a landing, like a SAC bomber
returning to Plattsburgh
after a day of patrolling the ozone.
Every teacup in the pantry rattles.

The solid and graceful bodies
of Nuthatches, perpetually
upside down, like Yogis . . .
and Slate-Colored Juncoes, feeding
on the ground, taking only
what falls to them.

The cats watch, one
from the lid of the breadbox,
another from the piano. A third
flexes its claws in sleep, dreaming

perhaps, of a chicken neck,
or of being worshiped as a god
at Bubastis, during
the XXIII dynasty.

The Circle on the Grass

1

Last night the wind came into the yard,
and wrenched the biggest branch
from the box elder, and threw it down
—no, that was not what it wanted—
and kept on going.

This morning a man arrives
with ladders, ropes and saws,
to cut down what is left.

2

Eighty years ago, someone
planted the sapling
midway between porch and fence,
and later that day,
looked down from the bedroom
on the highest branch.

The woman who stood at the window
could only imagine shade,
and the sound of leaves moving overhead,
like so many whispered conversations.

3

I keep busy in the house,
but I hear the high drone
of the saw, and the drop in pitch
as chain cuts into bark.

I clean with the vacuum
so I won't have to listen.
Finally the man goes for lunch,
leaving the house quiet
as a face paralyzed by strokes.

4

All afternoon I hear the blunt
shudder of limbs striking the ground.
The tree drops its arms
like someone abandoning a conviction:
—perhaps I have been wrong all this time—.

When it's over, there is nothing left
but a pale circle on the grass,
dark in the center, like an eye.

Falling

March. Rain. Five days now.
Water gathers in flat places,
finds every space between stones.
The river peaks, fish lie
stunned on the muddy bottom.

After the crash in the Swiss
countryside, an arm
dangles from a tree. A tortoiseshell
comb parts the grass.
The bookmark is still in place.

This month I was five days late,
but now the blood comes in a rush.
Let everything fall where it will.
Someone unpacks a suitcase, thinks
of living without possessions.

Afternoon in the House

It's quiet here. The cats
sprawl, each
in a favored place.
The geranium leans this way
to see if I'm writing about her:
head all petals, brown
stalks, and those green fans.
So you see,
I am writing about you.

I turn on the radio. Wrong.
Let's not have any noise
in this room, except
the sound of a voice reading a poem.
The cats request
The Meadow Mouse, by Theodore Roethke.

The house settles down on its haunches
for a doze.
I know you are with me, plants,
and cats—and even so, I'm frightened,
sitting in the middle of perfect
possibility.

Full Moon in Winter

Bare branches rise
and fall overhead.
The barn door bangs loose,
persistent as remorse
after anger and shouting.

Dogs bark across the pond.
The shadow of the house
appears on the crusted snow
like the idea of a house,
and my own shadow

lies down in the cold
at my feet, lunatic,
like someone tired
of living in a body,
needy and full of desire. . . .

After an Early Frost

The cat takes her squealing mouse into the bathtub to play. Monopoly? Twenty Questions? I hear bottles and brushes hitting the floor. Then nothing.

I go to take out the dead mouse.

Not in the tub. Nowhere on the floor. Suddenly the towel moves on the rack. The mouse crouches there, shaking, eyes wide, sides heaving, nose like a peppercorn.

I consider bringing the cat back to finish the job. I consider finishing the job myself.

Instead, I nudge it into a coffee can. I put the can under a bush in the garden and go off to write letters.

Maybe it will be back in the shed by suppertime, making a nest in the rag basket. Or I might find it under a leaf, rigid and shrunken. Who knows. Somebody will carry me out of here too, though not for a while.

Year Day

We are living together on the earth.
The clock's heart
beats in its wooden chest.
The cats follow the sun through the house.
We lie down together at night.

Today, you work in your office,
and I in my study. Sometimes
we are busy and casual.
Sitting here, I can see
the path we have made on the rug.

The hermit gives up
after thirty years of hiding in the jungle.
The last door to the last room
comes unlatched. Here are the gestures
of my hands. Wear them in your hair.

The Suitor

We lie back to back. Curtains
lift and fall,
like the chest of someone sleeping.
Wind moves the leaves of the box elder;
they show their light undersides,
turning all at once
like a school of fish.
Suddenly I understand that I am happy.
For months this feeling
has been coming closer, stopping
for short visits, like a timid suitor.

American Triptych

1 At the Store

Clumps of daffodils along the storefront
bend low this morning, late snow
pushing their bright heads down.
The flag snaps and tugs at the pole
beside the door.

The old freezer, full of Maine blueberries
and breaded scallops, mumbles along.
A box of fresh bananas on the floor,
luminous and exotic. . . .
I take what I need from the narrow aisles.

Cousins arrive like themes and variations.
Ansel leans on the counter,
remembering other late spring snows,
the blue snow of '32:
Yes, it *was,* it was *blue.*
Forrest comes and goes quickly
with a length of stovepipe, telling
about the neighbors' chimney fire.

The store is a bandstand. All our voices
sound from it, making the same motley
American music Ives heard;
this piece starting quietly,
with the repeated clink of a flagpole
pulley in the doorway of a country store.

2 Down the Road

Early summer. Sun low over the pond. Down the road the neighbors' children play baseball in the twilight. I see the ball leave the bat; a moment later the sound reaches me where I sit.

No deaths or separations, no disappointments in love. They are throwing and hitting the ball. Sometimes it arcs higher than the house, sometimes it tunnels into tall grass at the edge of the hayfield.

3 Potluck at the Wilmot Flat Baptist Church

We drive to the Flat on a clear November night. Stars and planets appear in the eastern sky, not yet in the west.

Voices rise from the social hall downstairs, the clink of silverware and plates, the smell of coffee.

As we walk into the room faces turn to us, friendly and curious. We are seated at the speakers' table, next to the town historian, a retired schoolteacher who is lively and precise.

The table is decorated with red, white, and blue streamers, and framed *Time* and *Newsweek* covers of the President, just elected. Someone has tied peanuts to small branches with red, white, and blue yarn, and set the branches upright in lumps of clay at the center of each table.

After the meal everyone clears food from the tables, and tables from the hall. Then we go up to the sanctuary, where my husband reads poems from the pulpit.

One woman looks out the window continually. I notice the altar cloth, tasseled and embroidered in gold thread: Till I Come. There is applause after each poem.

On the way home we pass the white clapboard faces of the library and town hall, luminous in the moonlight, and I remember the first time I ever voted—in a township hall in Michigan.

That same wonderful smell of coffee was in the air, and I found myself among people trying to live ordered lives. . . . And again I am struck with love for the Republic.

Now That We Live

Fat spider by the door.

Brow of hayfield, blue
eye of pond.
Sky at night like an open well.

Whip-Poor-Will calls
in the tall grass:
I belong to the Queen of Heaven!

The cheerful worm
in the cheerful ground.

Regular shape of meadow and wall
under the blue
              imperturbable mountain.

The Boat of Quiet Hours
(1986)

⸺ for Perkins

> And, as the year
> Grows lush in juicy stalks, I'll smoothly steer
> My little boat, for many quiet hours,
> With streams that deepen freshly into bowers.
>
> John Keats
> *Endymion, Book I*

I

Walking Alone in Late Winter

Evening at a Country Inn

From here I see a single red cloud
impaled on the Town Hall weather vane.
Now the horses are back in their stalls,
and the dogs are nowhere in sight
that made them run and buck
in the brittle morning light.

You laughed only once all day—
when the cat ate cucumbers
in Chekhov's story . . . and now you smoke
and pace the long hallway downstairs.

The cook is roasting meat for the evening meal,
and the smell rises to all the rooms.
Red-faced skiers stamp past you
on their way in; their hunger is Homeric.

I know you are thinking of the accident —
of picking the slivered glass from his hair.
Just now a truck loaded with hay
stopped at the village store to get gas.
I wish you would look at the hay—
the beautiful sane and solid bales of hay.

At the Town Dump

Sometimes I nod to my neighbor
as he flings lath and plaster or cleared
brush on the swelling pile. Talk
is impossible; the dozer shudders toward us,
flattening everything in its path.

Last March I got stuck in the mud.
Archie Portigue was there, thin
from the cancer that would kill him,
with his yellow pickup, its sides
akimbo from many loads. Archie
pushed as I rocked the car; the clutch
smelled hot; then with finesse
he jumped on the fender. . . . Saved,
I saw his small body in the rearview mirror
get smaller as he waved.

A boy pokes with a stick at a burnt-out
sofa cushion. . . . He brings the insides
out with clear delight. Near where I stand
the toe of a boot protrudes from the sand.

Today I brought the bug-riddled remains
of my garden. A single ripe tomato—last fruit,
immaculate—evaded harvest, and dangles
from a vine. I offer it to oblivion
with the rest of what was mine.

Killing the Plants

That year I discovered the virtues
of plants as companions: they don't
argue, they don't ask for much,
they don't stay out until 3:00 A.M., then
lie to you about where they've been. . . .

I can't summon the ambition
to repot this grape ivy, or this sad
old cactus, or even to move them out
onto the porch for the summer,
where their lives would certainly
improve. I give them
a grudging dash of water—that's all
they get. I wonder if they suspect

that like Hamlet I rehearse murder
all hours of the day and night,
considering the town dump
and compost pile as possible graves. . . .

The truth is that if I permit them
to live, they will go on giving
alms to the poor: sweet air, miraculous
flowers, the example of persistence.

The Painters

A hot dry day in early fall. . . .
The men have cut the vines
from the shutters, and scraped
the clapboards clean, and now
their heads appear all day
in all the windows . . .
their arms or shirtless torsos,
or a rainbow-speckled rag
swinging from a belt.

They work in earnest—
these are the last warm days.
Flies bump and buzz
between the screens and panes,
torpid from last night's frost:
the brittle months advance . . .
ruts frozen in the icy drive,
and the deeply black and soundless
nights. But now the painters

lean out from their ladders, squint
against the light, and lay on
the thick white paint.
From the lawn their radio predicts rain,
then cold Canadian air. . . .
One of them works way up
on the dormer peak,
where a few wasps levitate
near the vestige of a nest.

Back from the City

After three days and nights of rich food
and late talk in overheated rooms,
of walks between mounds of garbage
and human forms bedded down for the night
under rags, I come back to my dooryard,
to my own wooden step.

The last red leaves fall to the ground
and frost has blackened the herbs and asters
that grew beside the porch. The air
is still and cool, and the withered grass
lies flat in the field. A nuthatch spirals
down the rough trunk of the tree.

At the Cloisters I indulged in piety
while gazing at a painted lindenwood Pietà—
Mary holding her pierced and desiccated son
across her knees; but when a man stepped close
under the tasseled awning of the hotel,
asking for "a quarter for someone
down on his luck," I quickly turned my back.

Now I hear tiny bits of bark and moss
break off under the bird's beak and claw,
and fall onto already-fallen leaves.
"Do you love me?" said Christ to his disciple.
"Lord, you know
that I love you."
                "Then feed my sheep."

Deer Season

November, late afternoon. I'm driving fast,
only the parking lights on.
A minor infringement of the law. . . .

All along Route 4 men wearing orange
step out of the woods after a day
of hunting, their rifles pointed
toward the ground.
                        The sky turns red, then
purple in the west, and the luminous
birches lean over the narrow macadam road.

I cross the little bridge
near the pool called The Pork Barrel,
where the best fishing is,
and pass the Fentons' farm—the windows
of the milking parlor bright, the great
silver cooling tank beginning to chill the milk.

I've seen the veal calves drink from pails
in their stalls. Suppose even the ear of wheat
suffers in the mill. . . .
Moving fast in my car at dusk
I plan our evening meal.

November Calf

She calved in the ravine, beside
the green-scummed pond.
Full clouds and mist hung low—
it was unseasonably warm. Steam
rose from her head as she pushed
and called; her cries went out
over the still-lush fields.

First came the front feet, then
the blossom-nose, shell-pink
and glistening; and then the broad
forehead, flopping black ears,
and neck. . . . She worked
until the steaming length of him
rushed out onto the ground, then
turned and licked him with her wide
pink tongue. He lifted up his head
and looked around.

The herd pressed close to see, then
frolicked up the bank, flicking
their tails. It looked like revelry.
The farmer set off for the barn,
swinging in a widening arc
a frayed and knotted scrap of rope.

The Beaver Pool in December

The brook is still open
where the water falls,
but over the deeper pools
clear ice forms; over the dark
shapes of stones, a rotting log,
and amber leaves that clattered down
after the first heavy frost.

Though I wait in the cold
until dusk, and though a sudden
bubble of air rises under the ice,
I see not a single animal.

The beavers thrive somewhere
else, eating the bark of hoarded
saplings. How they struggled
to pull the long branches
over the stiffening bank . . .

but now they pass without
effort, all through the chilly
water; moving like thoughts
in an unconflicted mind.

Apple Dropping into Deep Early Snow

A jay settled on a branch, making it sway.
The one shriveled fruit that remained
gave way to the deepening drift below.
I happened to see it the moment it fell.

Dusk is eager and comes early. A car
creeps over the hill. Still in the dark I try
to tell if I am numbered with the damned,
who cry, outraged, *Lord, when did we see You?*

Drink, Eat, Sleep

I never drink from this blue tin cup
speckled with white
without thinking of stars on a clear,
cold night—of Venus blazing low
over the leafless trees; and Canis
great and small—dogs without flesh,
fur, blood, or bone . . . dogs made of light,
apparitions of cold light, with black
and trackless spaces in between. . . .
The angel gave a little book
to the prophet, telling him to eat—
eat and tell of the end of time.
Strange food, infinitely strange,
but the pages were like honey
to his tongue. . . .

Rain in January

I woke before dawn, still
in a body. Water ran
down every window, and rushed
from the eaves.

Beneath the empty feeder
a skunk was prowling for suet
or seed. The lamps flickered off
and then came on again.

Smoke from the chimney
could not rise. It came down
into the yard, and brooded there
on the unlikelihood of reaching

heaven. When my arm slipped
from the arm of the chair
I let it hang beside me, pale,
useless, and strange.

Depression in Winter

There comes a little space between the south
side of a boulder
and the snow that fills the woods around it.
Sun heats the stone, reveals
a crescent of bare ground: brown ferns,
and tufts of needles like red hair,
acorns, a patch of moss, bright green. . . .

I sank with every step up to my knees,
throwing myself forward with a violence
of effort, greedy for unhappiness—
until by accident I found the stone,
with its secret porch of heat and light,
where something small could luxuriate, then
turned back down my path, chastened and calm.

Bright Sun after Heavy Snow

A ledge of ice slides from the eaves,
piercing the crusted drift. Astonishing
how even a little violence
eases the mind.

In this extreme state of light
everything seems flawed: the streaked
pane, the forced bulbs on the sill
that refuse to bloom. . . . A wad of dust
rolls like a desert weed
over the drafty floor.

Again I recall a neighbor's
small affront—it rises in my mind
like the huge banks of snow along the road:
the plow, passing up and down all day,
pushes them higher and higher. . . .

The shadow of smoke rising from the chimney
moves abruptly over the yard.
The clothesline rises in the wind. One
wooden pin is left, solitary as a finger;
it, too, rises and falls.

Ice Storm

For the hemlocks and broad-leafed evergreens
a beautiful and precarious state of being. . . .
Here in the suburbs of New Haven
nature, unrestrained, lops the weaker limbs
of shrubs and trees with a sense of aesthetics
that is practical and sinister. . . .

I am a guest in this house.
On the bedside table *Good Housekeeping,* and
A Nietzsche Reader. . . .The others are still asleep.
The most painful longing comes over me.
A longing not of the body. . . .

It could be for beauty—
I mean what Keats was panting after,
for which I love and honor him;
it could be for the promises of God;
or for oblivion, *nada;* or some condition even more
extreme, which I intuit, but can't quite name.

Walking Alone in Late Winter

How long the winter has lasted—like a Mahler
symphony, or an hour in the dentist's chair.
In the fields the grasses are matted
and gray, making me think of June, when hay
and vetch burgeon in the heat, and warm rain
swells the globed buds of the peony.

Ice on the pond breaks into huge planes. One
sticks like a barge gone awry at the neck
of the bridge. . . .The reeds
and shrubby brush along the shore
gleam with ice that shatters when the breeze
moves them. From beyond the bog
the sound of water rushing over trees
felled by the zealous beavers,
who bring them crashing down. . . . Sometimes
it seems they do it just for fun.

Those days of anger and remorse
come back to me; you fidgeting with your ring,
sliding it off, then jabbing it on again.

The wind is keen coming over the ice;
it carries the sound of breaking glass.
And the sun, bright but not warm,
has gone behind the hill. Chill, or the fear
of chill, sends me hurrying home.

II

Mud Season

The Hermit

The meeting ran needlessly late,
and while yawns were suppressed around the room
the river swelled until it spilled.
When the speaker finished, I made for the car
and home as fast as fog would allow—
until I came upon a barricade: beyond,
black pools eddied over the road. Detour.
The last familiar thing I saw: the steaming
heaps of bark beside the lumber mill.

No other cars on the narrow, icy lane; no house
or barn for miles, until the lights of a Christmas tree
shone from the small windows of a trailer.
And then I knew I couldn't be far
from the East Village and the main road.
I was terribly wide awake. . . .

To calm myself I thought of drinking water
at the kitchen sink, in the circle of light
the little red lamp makes in the evening . . .
of half-filling a second glass
and splashing it into the dish of white narcissus
growing on the sill. In China
this flower is called the hermit,
and people greet the turning of the year
with bowls of freshly opened blossoms. . . .

The Pond at Dusk

A fly wounds the water but the wound
soon heals. Swallows tilt and twitter
overhead, dropping now and then toward
the outward-radiating evidence of food.

The green haze on the trees changes
into leaves, and what looks like smoke
floating over the neighbor's barn
is only apple blossoms.

But sometimes what looks like disaster
is disaster: the day comes at last,
and the men struggle with the casket
just clearing the pews.

High Water

Eight days of rain;
the ground refuses more.
My neighbors are morose at the village store.

I'm sick of holding still, sick of indoors,
so I walk through the heavy-headed grasses
to watch the river reach
for the bridge's wooden planks,
bending the lithe swamp maples
that grow along the banks.

Nothing but trouble comes to mind
as I lean over the rusty iron rail.
I know of plenty, in detail, that is not
my own. I nudge a pebble over the edge.
It drops with a *thunk* into the water—
dark, voluminous, and clear,
and moving headlong away from here.

Evening Sun

Why does this light force me back
to my childhood? I wore a yellow
summer dress, and the skirt
made a perfect circle.

               Turning and turning
until it flared to the limit
was irresistible. . . .The grass and trees,
my outstretched arms, and the skirt
whirled in the ochre light
of an early June evening.

               And I knew then
that I would have to live, and go on
living: what a sorrow it was; and still
what sorrow burns
but does not destroy my heart.

Summer 1890: Near the Gulf

The hour was late, and the others
were asleep. He struck a match
on the wooden railing of the porch
and lit a cigarette

while she beheld his head and hand,
estranged from the body
in wavering light. . . .

What she felt then
would, like heavy wind
and rain, bring
any open flower to the ground.

He let the spent match
fall; but the face remained
before her, like a bright light
before a closed eye. . . .

Photograph of a Child on a Vermont Hillside

Beside the rocking horse, for which
she has grown too large,
and the shirts that hang still on the line,
she looks down.
The face is dour and pale
with something private, and will not admit
the journalist, up from Boston
for country color.

How well she knows these hills—
green receding unaccountably to blue—
and the low meadow in middle distance,
buff-colored now, with one
misshapen tree. . . .

What would she say if she cared
to speak a word? a word meaning
childhood is woe in solitude,
and the bliss of turning circles
barefoot in the dusty drive
after the supper dishes are done. . . .

What Came to Me

I took the last
dusty piece of china
out of the barrel.
It was your gravy boat,
with a hard, brown
drop of gravy still
on the porcelain lip.
I grieved for you then
as I never had before.

Main Street: Tilton, New Hampshire

I waited in the car while he
went into the small old-fashioned grocery
for a wedge of cheddar.

Late summer, Friday afternoon.
A mother and child walked past
trading mock blows
with paper bags full of—what —
maybe new clothes for school.
They turned the corner by the Laundromat,
and finally even the heel
of the girl's rubber flip-flop
passed from sight.

Across the street a blue pickup, noisy,
with some kind of homemade wooden
scaffolding in the bed, pulled
close to the curb. A man got out
and entered the bank. . . .
                            A woman sat
in the cab, dabbing her face
with a tissue. She might have been weeping,
but it was hot and still,
and maybe she wasn't weeping at all.

Through time and space we came
to Main Street—three days before
Labor Day, 1984, 4:47 in the afternoon;
and then that moment passed, displaced
by others equally equivocal.

Teacher

Sometimes there's gravel on the bend
by Vernondale's Store in North Sutton.
I've learned to watch for that,
and for the German shepherd
who lies in the road
at the foot of his master's drive.

I've seen the farm-market signs
change with the weather: *Potatoes,*
to *Pumpkins,* to *Firewood: Inquire Within.*

My students have stayed the same.
They still cut class to go skiing
or fix their cars,
and they continue to write:
. . . his flowing mane and proud bearing
are timeless symbols of the pure blood
coursing through his royal veins. . . .

Today the marsh is white with ice.
The reeds look brittle and defeated.
While I was at work
someone covered the three poplars
by that cottage porch; wrapped them
in canvas against ice and wind,
then cinched the canvas with ropes,
making waists for the three lithe caryatids,
who seem to be holding up the roof
while they wait for April thaw. . . .

Frost Flowers

Sap withdraws from the upper reaches
of maples; the squirrel digs deeper
and deeper in the moss
to bury the acorns that fall
all around, distracting him.

I'm out here in the dusk,
tired from teaching and a little drunk,
where the wild asters, last blossoms
of the season, straggle uphill.
Frost flowers, I've heard them called.
The white ones have yellow centers
at first: later they darken
to a rosy copper. They're mostly done.
Then the blue ones come on. It's blue
all around me now, though the color
has gone with the sun.

My sarcasm wounded a student today.
Afterward I heard him running down the stairs.

There is no one at home but me—
and I'm not at home; I'm up here on the hill,
looking at the dark windows below.
Let them be dark. Some large bird
calls down-mountain—a cry
astonishingly loud, distressing. . . .

I was cruel to him: it is a bitter thing.
The air is damp and cold,

and by now I am a little hungry. . . .
The squirrel is high in the oak,
gone to his nest, and night has silenced
the last loud rupture of the calm.

The Sandy Hole

The infant's coffin no bigger than a flightbag. . . .
The young father steps backward from the sandy hole,
eyes wide and dry, his hand over his mouth.
No one dares to come near him, even to touch his sleeve.

Depression

. . . a mote. A little world. Dusty. Dusty.
The universe is dust. Who can bear it?
Christ comes. The women feed him, bathe his feet
with tears, bring spices, find the empty tomb,
burst out to tell the men, are not believed. . . .

Sun and Moon

for Donald Clark

Drugged and drowsy but not asleep
I heard my blind roommate's daughter
helping her with her meal:
"What's that? Squash?"
"No. It's spinach."

Back from a brain-scan, she dozed
to the sound of the Soaps: adultery,
amnesia, shady business deals,
and long, white hospital halls. . . .
No separation between life and art.

I heard two nurses whispering:
Mr. Malcomson had died.
An hour later one of them came to say
that a private room was free.

A chill spring breeze
perturbed the plastic drape.
I lay back on the new bed,
and had a vision of souls
stacked up like pelts
under my soul, which was ill—
so heavy with grief
it kept the others from rising.

No varicolored tubes
serpentined beneath the covers;
I had the vital signs of a healthy,

early-middle-aged woman.
There was nothing to cut or dress,
remove or replace.

A week of stupor. Sun and moon
rose and set over the small enclosed
court, the trees. . . .
The doctor's face appeared
and disappeared
over the foot of the bed. By slow degrees
the outlandish sadness waned.

Restored to my living room
I looked at the tables, chairs, and pictures
with something like delight,
only pale, faint—as from a great height.
I let the phone ring; the mail
accrued unopened
on the table in the hall.

Whirligigs

Two bearded men: one chops a log,
the other milks a cow. Even at night
they turn their backsides to the strongest
gusts and work like mad, but never
finish, though they bend over the same log
and the same cow for the third year
in a row.

        They winter in the cellar,
near the apple-cider kegs. For all I know
they take a nip or two, pass stories back
and forth with a speckled tinware cup.

Come spring I reinstate them
on weathered poles among the scilla
and early daffodils. I think they must be
brothers. . . and we three make a family,
waving our arms to scare the crows away.

February: Thinking of Flowers

Now wind torments the field,
turning the white surface back
on itself, back and back on itself,
like an animal licking a wound.

Nothing but white—the air, the light;
only one brown milkweed pod
bobbing in the gully, smallest
brown boat on the immense tide.

A single green sprouting thing
would restore me. . . .

Then think of the tall delphinium,
swaying, or the bee when it comes
to the tongue of the burgundy lily.

Portrait of a Figure near Water

Rebuked, she turned and ran
uphill to the barn. Anger, the inner
arsonist, held a match to her brain.
She observed her life: against her will
it survived the unwavering flame.

The barn was empty of animals.
Only a swallow tilted
near the beams, and bats
hung from the rafters
the roof sagged between.

Her breath became steady
where, years past, the farmer cooled
the big tin amphorae of milk.
The stone trough was still
filled with water: she watched it
and received its calm.

So it is when we retreat in anger:
we think we burn alone
and there is no balm.
Then water enters, though it makes
no sound.

Mud Season

Here in purgatory bare ground
is visible, except in shady places
where snow prevails.

Still, each day sees
the restoration of another animal:
a sparrow, just now a sleepy wasp;
and, at twilight, the skunk
pokes out of the den,
anxious for mates and meals. . . .

On the floor of the woodshed
the coldest imaginable ooze,
and soon the first shoots
of asparagus will rise,
the fingers of Lazarus. . . .

Earth's open wounds—where the plow
gouged the ground last November—
must be smoothed; some sown
with seed, and all forgotten.

Now the nuthatch spurns the suet,
resuming its diet of flies, and the mesh
bag, limp and greasy, might be taken
down.

Beside the porch step
the crocus prepares an exaltation
of purple, but for the moment
holds its tongue. . . .

III

The Boat of Quiet Hours

Thinking of Madame Bovary

The first hot April day the granite step
was warm. Flies droned in the grass.
When a car went past they rose
in unison, then dropped back down. . . .

I saw that a yellow crocus bud had pierced
a dead oak leaf, then opened wide. How strong
its appetite for the luxury of the sun!

Everyone longs for love's tense joys and red delights.

And then I spied an ant
dragging a ragged, disembodied wing
up the warm brick walk. It must have been
the Methodist in me that leaned forward,
preceded by my shadow, to put a twig just where
the ant was struggling with its own desire.

April Walk

Evening came, and work was done.
We went for a walk to see
what winter had exacted
from our swimming place on the pond.

The moss was immoderately green,
and spongy underfoot; stepping on it seemed
a breach of etiquette.
We found our picnic table
sitting squarely in the bog—only
a minor prank. The slender birches watched us
leaning from the bank.

And where the river launches forth
from the south end of the pond
the water coursed high and clear
under the little bridge.
Huge, suspended in the surge, grand-
father turtle moved sporadically
one flat, prehistoric, clawed arm
at a time, keeping his head downstream.

Years ago he made a vow
not to be agitated by the runnels
of spring, the abundance of light,
warm wind smelling of rain,
or the peepers' throstling. . . .

We watched till he was out of sight
and seemed illusory, then turned
toward home—the windows
brazen in the setting sun. . . .

Philosophy in Warm Weather

Now all the doors and windows
are open, and we move so easily
through the rooms. Cats roll
on the sunny rugs, and a clumsy wasp
climbs the pane, pausing
to rub a leg over her head.

All around physical life reconvenes.
The molecules of our bodies must love
to exist: they whirl in circles
and seem to begrudge us nothing.
Heat, Horatio, *heat* makes them
put this antic disposition on!

This year's brown spider
sways over the door as I come
and go. A single poppy shouts
from the far field, and the crow,
beyond alarm, goes right on
pulling up the corn.

No Steps

The young bull dropped his head and stared.
Only a wispy wire—electrified—kept us
apart. That, and two long rows of asparagus.
An ancient apple tree
blossomed prodigally pink and white.

The muddy path sucked at my shoe,
but I reached the granite step, and knocked
at the rickety porch door.
Deep in the house a dog began to bark.
I had prepared my Heart Fund speech,
and the first word—*When*—was on my tongue.

I heard no steps—only the breeze
riffling the tender poplar leaves,
and a random, meditative *moo*
behind me. . . . Relieved, I turned back
to the car, passing once more
under the bull's judicial eye. . . .
Everything was intact: the canister,
still far too light and mute,
and metal boutonnières where they began—
in a zip-lock plastic sandwich bag.

Wash

All day the blanket snapped and swelled
on the line, roused by a hot spring wind. . . .
From there it witnessed the first sparrow,
early flies lifting their sticky feet,
and a green haze on the south-sloping hills.
Clouds rode over the mountain. . . . At dusk
I took the blanket in, and we slept,
restless, under its fragrant weight.

Inertia

My head was heavy, heavy;
so was the atmosphere.
I had to ask two times
before my hand would scratch my ear.
I thought I should be out
and doing! The grass, for one thing,
needed mowing.

Just then a centipede
reared from the spine
of my open dictionary. It tried
the air with enterprising feelers,
then made its way along the gorge
between 202 and 203. *The valley
of the shadow of death* came to mind
inexorably.

It can't be easy for the left hand
to know what the right is doing.
And how, on such a day, when the sky
is hazy and perfunctory, how does it
get itself started without feeling
muddled and heavy-hearted?

Well, it had its fill of etymology.
I watched it pull its tail
over the edge of the page, and vanish
in a pile of mail.

Camp Evergreen

The boats like huge bright birds
sail back when someone calls them:
the small campers struggle out
and climb the hill to lunch.
I see the last dawdler
disappear in a ridge of trees.

The whole valley sighs
in the haze and heat of noon. Far out
a fish astonishes the air, falls back
into its element. From the marshy cove
the bullfrog offers thoughts
on the proper limits of ambition.

An hour passes. Piano music
comes floating over the water, falters,
begins again, falters. . . .
Only work will make it right.

Some small thing I can't quite see
clatters down through the leafy dome.
Now it is high summer: the solstice:
longed-for, possessed, luxurious, and sad.

The Appointment

The phoebe flew back and forth
between the fencepost and the tree—
not nest-building, just restlessly . . .
and I heard the motorboat on the lake,
going around and through its own wake,
towing the campers two by two.

I thought of a dozen things to do
but rejected them all
in favor of fretting about you.
It might have been the finest day of summer—
the hay was rich and dry, and the breeze
made the heart-shaped leaves of the birch
tell all their secrets,
though they were lost on me. . . .

Bees rummaged through the lilies, methodical
as thieves in a chest of drawers.
I saw them from the chair
nearest the cool foundation stones.
Out of the cellar window came
a draught of damp and evil-smelling air.

The potted geraniums on the porch
hung limp in the blaze of noon. I could
not stir to water them. If you
had turned into the drive just then, even
with cheerful news, I doubt
I could have heard what you had to say.

Sick at Summer's End

Today from the darkened room I heard
the men across the lake, taking up the dock
for winter. They stacked the clattering sections
well up the sandy slope, then
shedded the canoes; I suppose
they left the cabins locked.

Late afternoon the paper carrier's car
slowed on the blacktop, stopped,
and, flinging gravel, started up again.

I know the garden ramps and goes
to seed. And the blue jay chills
with its call that sounds like the butcher's
saw when it cuts into bone.
The room turns darker still
by insensible degrees, and crickets
shrill from the window well. . . .

I'm falling upward, nothing to hold me down.

Alone for a Week

I washed a load of clothes
and hung them out to dry.
Then I went up to town
and busied myself all day.
The sleeve of your best shirt
rose ceremonious
when I drove in; our night-
clothes twined and untwined in
a little gust of wind.

For me it was getting late;
for you, where you were, not.
The harvest moon was full
but sparse clouds made its light
not quite reliable.
The bed on your side seemed
as wide and flat as Kansas;
your pillow plump, cool,
and allegorical. . . .

The Bat

I was reading about rationalism,
the kind of thing we do up north
in early winter, where the sun
leaves work for the day at 4:15.

Maybe the world *is* intelligible
to the rational mind;
and maybe we light the lamps at dusk
for nothing. . . .

Then I heard wings overhead.

The cats and I chased the bat
in circles—living room, kitchen,
pantry, kitchen, living room. . . .
At every turn it evaded us

like the identity of the third person
in the Trinity: the one
who spoke through the prophets,
the one who astounded Mary
by suddenly coming near.

Siesta: Barbados

From bed we heard
the gardener move down the hedge
of oleander, chopping out the weeds
with her long, curved cutlass
and singing. A lizard gripped the coarse
stucco of the ceiling. It pulsed;
it cocked its head; and when the blade
rang out against a stone
it flicked its question-mark of a tail
around to the other side. . . .
Sea breeze swelled the curtain,
and tried the shuttered door. . .
and then you reached for the hem
of my red dress with blue leaves
and lemon lilies—the one you bought for me
from the woman who came to our porch
balancing a bundle on her head.

Trouble with Math in a One-Room Country School

The others bent their heads and started in.
Confused, I asked my neighbor
to explain—a sturdy, bright-cheeked girl
who brought raw milk to school from her family's
herd of Holsteins. Ann had a blue bookmark,
and on it Christ revealed his beating heart,
holding the flesh back with His wounded hand.
Ann understood division. . . .

Miss Moran sprang from her monumental desk
and led me roughly through the class
without a word. My shame was radical
as she propelled me past the cloakroom
to the furnace closet, where only the boys
were put, only the older ones at that.
The door swung briskly shut.

The warmth, the gloom, the smell
of sweeping compound clinging to the broom
soothed me. I found a bucket, turned it
upside down, and sat, hugging my knees.
I hummed a theme from Haydn that I knew
from my piano lessons . . .
and hardened my heart against authority.
And then I heard her steps, her fingers
on the latch. She led me, blinking
and changed, back to the class.

The Little Boat

As soon as spring peepers sounded from the stream
and boggy lower barnyard across the road
Mother let us bring out the cots,
and sleeping bags—red and gray and black
plaid flannel, still smelling of the cedar chest.

How hard it was to settle down that first night
out on the big screened porch: three times
trains passed the crossing, and the peepers' song
was lost under the whistle (two long,
two short), the rumble and clacking,
and clang of the crossing bell. The neighbor's
cocker spaniel howled the whole time
and for a full two minutes after. . . . Or rain
sluiced from the eaves, and we saw black limbs
against a sky whitened by lightning.
The gloom was lavish and agreeable. . . .

August came. Mother took us to Wahr's on State Street,
bought each of us a reader, speller, Big 10 Tablet,
a bottle of amber glue with a slit like a closed eye,
pencils, erasers of a violent pink, a penmanship workbook
for practicing loops that looked to me
like the culvert under the road, whose dark and webby length
Brother and I dared each other to run through . . .
and crayons, the colors ranging from one to another
until what began as yellow ended amazingly as blue.

One morning we walked to the top of Foster Road,
and stood under the Reimers' big maple.
Ground fog rose from the hay stubble.

We heard gears grinding at the foot of the hill;
the bus appeared and we knew we had to get in.
All day in my imagination my body floated
above the classroom, navigating easily
between fluorescent shoals. . . . I was listening,
floating, watching. . . . The others stayed below
at their desks (I saw the crown of my own head
bending over a book), and no one knew I was not
where I seemed to be. . . .

IV

Things

Song

An oriole sings from the hedge
and in the hotel kitchen
the chef sweetens cream for pastries.
Far off, lightning and thunder agree
to join us for a few days
here in the valley. How lucky we are
to be holding hands on a porch
in the country. But even this
is not the joy that trembles
under every leaf and tongue.

At the Summer Solstice

Noon heat. And later, hotter still. . . .
The neighbor's son rides up and down the field
turning the hay—turning it with flourishes.

The tractor dips into the low clovery place
where melt from the mountain
comes down in the spring, and wild
lupine grows. Only the boy's blond head
can be seen; but then he comes smartly
up again—to whirl, deft, around
the pear tree near the barn. Bravo . . .

bravissimo. The tall grass lies—cut,
turned, raked, and dry. Later his father
comes down the lane with the baler. I hear
the steady thumping all afternoon.

So hot, so hot today. . . . I will stay in our room
with the shades drawn, waiting for you
to come with sleepy eyes, and pass your fingers
lightly, lightly up my thighs.

Coming Home at Twilight in Late Summer

We turned into the drive,
and gravel flew up from the tires
like sparks from a fire. So much
to be done—the unpacking, the mail
and papers . . . the grass needed mowing. . . .
We climbed stiffly out of the car.
The shut-off engine ticked as it cooled.

And then we noticed the pear tree,
the limbs so heavy with fruit
they nearly touched the ground.
We went out to the meadow; our steps
made black holes in the grass;
and we each took a pear,
and ate, and were grateful.

The Visit

The talkative guest has gone,
and we sit in the yard
saying nothing. The slender moon
comes over the peak of the barn.

The air is damp, and dense
with the scent of honeysuckle. . . .
The last clever story has been told
and answered with laughter.

With my sleeping self I met
my obligations, but now I am aware
of the silence, and your affection,
and the delicate sadness of dusk.

Parents' Weekend: Camp Kenwood

Midmorning the company of cars
began to cross the little bridge;
the loose plank knocked and knocked.
The dog established her front feet
on the fence and barked.

Now the *pock-pick-pock* of tennis
floats over the lake, and the slap
of the ball when it hits the tape . . .
or children's voices singing
and prolonged applause. The breeze

comes from the south, is seasonably warm,
exciting the water to a bright confusion.
Once we set off for the woods
with little silver berry pails; then
everything seemed right just as it was. . . .

Reading Late of the Death of Keats

I tried to distract myself by reading
late, but the rhythmic whirr and puff
of the oxygen machine reached me
where I lay, in the room
that was mine in childhood.

Clearly I had packed the wrong book
in my haste: Keats died, propped up
to get more air. Severn
straightened the body on the bed,
and cut three dampened curls
from Keats's head.

A huge moth bumped against the screen,
tattering its wings. I turned
off the lamp and lay, all ears,
until it flew or fell away. . . .

Inpatient

The young attendants wrapped him in a red
velour blanket, and pulled the strapping taut.
Sedated on the stretcher and outside
for the last time, he raised his head and sniffed
the air like an animal. A wedge of geese
flew honking over us. The sky leaned close;
a drop of rain fell on his upturned face.
I stood aside, steward of Grandma's red-
letter New Testament and an empty vase.
The nurse went with him through the sliding door.
Without having to speak of it we left
the suitcase with his streetclothes in the car.

Campers Leaving: Summer 1981

Just now two chartered buses from Boston
pulled majestically onto Route 4. Dust
settled along the back road . . . the dog
stopped barking, turned three circles,
and lay back down.

Faces in every tinted window
turned back for one last look
at Ragged Mountain.
The sun had cleared the peak . . .
it was so bright they had to turn away. Soon
the noisy reconstruction of every family. . . .

Yesterday the phone rang at noon.
Father, calling from the hospital, had
something on his irradiated mind—just what,
he couldn't say, not that he didn't try.
He wept, and gave the phone to Mother
to say good-bye.

All summer I watched the campers from the far
shore. They learned to swim and sail,
and how to cling to a tipped canoe. Some
struggled the entire time but failed.
On the last day I heard a voice
say simply, *I need the pole.*
Sometimes when the wind is right it seems
that every word has been spoken to me.

Travel: After a Death

We drove past farms, the hills terraced with sheep.
A rook flapped upward from the stubbled corn:
its shadow fell across my lap one instant
and then was gone. The car was warm. Sleepy,
we passed through Devonshire: sun and showers. . . .
Fields, emerald in January, shone
through leafless hedges, and I watched a man
grasping his plaid cloth cap and walking stick
in one hand, while with perfect courtesy
he sent his dog before him through the stile,
bowing a little like a maître d'.

We found a room in a cold seaside hotel.
The manager had left a sullen girl
—no more than eighteen—and a parakeet
to run his business while he sunned himself
in Portugal. We watched her rip the key
from the wall and fling it toward us. Why,
I wondered, was the front door wedged open
in January, with a raw sea wind
blowing the woolen skirts of the townswomen,
who passed with market baskets on their arms,
their bodies bent forward against the chill
and the steep angle of the cobbled hill?

There were two urns of painted porcelain
flanking the door. A man could stand in one
and still have room for ashes . . . though he'd have
to be a strange man, like the poet Donne,
who pulled a shroud around himself and called

someone to draw—from life—his deathbed scene;
or like Turgenev, who saw bones and skulls
instead of Londoners walking the streets. . . .
Oh, when am I going to own my mind again?

Yard Sale

Under the stupefying sun
my family's belongings lie on the lawn
or heaped on borrowed card tables
in the gloom of the garage. Platters,
frying pans, our dead dog's
dish, box upon box of sheet music,
a wad of my father's pure linen
hand-rolled handkerchiefs, and his books
on the subsistence farm, a dream
for which his constitution ill suited him.

My niece dips seashells
in a glass of Coke. Sand streaks giddily
between bubbles to the bottom. Brown runnels
seem to scar her arm. "Do something silly!"
she begs her aunt. Listless,
I put a lampshade on my head.
Not good enough.

My brother takes pity on her
and they go walking together along the river
in places that seemed numinous
when we were five and held hands
with our young parents.
                                    She comes back
triumphant, with a plastic pellet box the size
of a bar of soap, which her father has clipped
to the pouch of her denim overalls. In it,
a snail with a slate-blue shell, and a few
blades of grass to make it feel at home. . . .

Hours pass. We close the metal strongbox
and sit down, stunned by divestiture.
What would he say? My niece
produces drawings and hands them over shyly:

a house with flowers, family
standing shoulder to shoulder
near the door under an affable sun,
and one she calls "Ghost with Long Legs."

Siesta: Hotel Frattina

Midafternoon the sound of weeping in the hall
woke me . . . hurried steps on the stair, and a door
slamming. I put on my glasses and stared
at nothing in particular.

We had walked all morning in the Forum
among pillars, cornices, and tilting
marble floors . . . armless torsos, faces
missing their noses—all fallen awry
among the grassy knolls.

Lord Byron brooded there on his love
for Teresa Guiccioli, only nineteen,
and someone else's wife. Oh, Siren Italy.

Just then the faucet gasped.
The ceiling seemed incalculably far away.
My mind revolted at all I had bought
in the chic little alleyways of Rome.

I longed for home, and the high collars we wear
a hundred miles north of the place
where Hawthorne wrote *The Scarlet Letter.*

I even longed to be bored again,
watching the pale sun rush—all business—
over the edge of the western world
by four on a November afternoon.

After Traveling

While in silence I rake
my plot of grass under the great trees—
the oaks and monumental maples—
I think of the proprietor

of the Caffè dei Fiori, sleepy, preoccupied,
dressed to the nines,
setting out tables in the Via Frattina—
extending his empire each day
by the smallest of increments
until there is room for another place . . .

at which we happen to be sitting
on the day the city official comes,
also dressed to the nines, to unwind
his shining metal measure in the street:
two tables must go. But for now
the proprietor shrugs, and a look
of infinite weariness passes
over his face. This is Rome:
remorse would be anomalous. . . .

And the white-coated waiters
arrange on doilied silver trays
the tiers of sugared pastries: angel wings,
cat tongues, and little kiwi tarts;
and the coffee machines fizzle and spurt
such appetizing steam; and a woman
in a long red cape goes by
leading a matched pair of pugs
on a bifurcated leash.

Twilight: After Haying

Yes, long shadows go out
from the bales; and yes, the soul
must part from the body:
what else could it do?

The men sprawl near the baler,
too tired to leave the field.
They talk and smoke,
and the tips of their cigarettes
blaze like small roses
in the night air. (It arrived
and settled among them
before they were aware.)

The moon comes
to count the bales,
and the dispossessed—
Whip-poor-will, Whip-poor-will
—sings from the dusty stubble.

These things happen . . . the soul's bliss
and suffering are bound together
like the grasses. . . .

The last, sweet exhalations
of timothy and vetch
go out with the song of the bird;
the ravaged field
grows wet with dew.

Who

These lines are written
by an animal, an angel,
a stranger sitting in my chair;
by someone who already knows
how to live without trouble
among books, and pots and pans. . . .

Who is it who asks me to find
language for the sound
a sheep's hoof makes when it strikes
a stone? And who speaks
the words which are my food?

Briefly It Enters, and Briefly Speaks

I am the blossom pressed in a book,
found again after two hundred years. . . .

I am the maker, the lover, and the keeper. . . .

When the young girl who starves
sits down to a table
she will sit beside me. . . .

I am food on the prisoner's plate. . . .

I am water rushing to the wellhead,
filling the pitcher until it spills. . . .

I am the patient gardener
of the dry and weedy garden. . . .

I am the stone step,
the latch, and the working hinge. . . .

I am the heart contracted by joy . . .
the longest hair, white
before the rest. . . .

I am there in the basket of fruit
presented to the widow. . . .

I am the musk rose opening
unattended, the fern on the boggy summit. . . .

I am the one whose love
overcomes you, already with you
when you think to call my name. . . .

Things

The hen flings a single pebble aside
with her yellow, reptilian foot.
Never in eternity the same sound—
a small stone falling on a red leaf.

The juncture of twig and branch,
scarred with lichen, is a gate
we might enter, singing.

The mouse pulls batting
from a hundred-year-old quilt.
She chewed a hole in a blue star
to get it, and now she thrives. . . .
Now is her time to thrive.

Things: simply lasting, then
failing to last: water, a blue heron's
eye, and the light passing
between them: into light all things
must fall, glad at last to have fallen.

Let Evening Come
(1990)

⸺ for Pauline Kenyon

So strange, life is. Why people do not
go around in a continual state of surprise
is beyond me.

William Maxwell

Three Songs at the End of Summer

A second crop of hay lies cut
and turned. Five gleaming crows
search and peck between the rows.
They make a low, companionable squawk,
and like midwives and undertakers
possess a weird authority.

Crickets leap from the stubble,
parting before me like the Red Sea.
The garden sprawls and spoils.

Across the lake the campers have learned
to water-ski. They have, or they haven't.
Sounds of the instructor's megaphone
suffuse the hazy air. "Relax! Relax!"

Cloud shadows rush over drying hay,
fences, dusty lane, and railroad ravine.
The first yellowing fronds of goldenrod
brighten the margins of the woods.

Schoolbooks, carpools, pleated skirts;
water, silver-still, and a vee of geese.

~

The cicada's dry monotony breaks
over me. The days are bright
and free, bright and free.

Then why did I cry today
for an hour, with my whole
body, the way babies cry?

      ~

A white, indifferent morning sky,
and a crow, hectoring from its nest
high in the hemlock, a nest as big
as a laundry basket . . .
                      In my childhood
I stood under a dripping oak,
while autumnal fog eddied around my feet,
waiting for the school bus
with a dread that took my breath away.

The damp dirt road gave off
this same complex organic scent.

I had the new books—words, numbers,
and operations with numbers I did not
comprehend—and crayons, unspoiled
by use, in a blue canvas satchel
with red leather straps.

Spruce, inadequate, and alien
I stood at the side of the road.
It was the only life I had.

After the Hurricane

I walk the fibrous woodland path to the pond.
Acorns break from the oaks, drop
through amber autumn air
which does not stir. The dog runs way ahead.

I find him snuffling on the shore
among water weeds that detached in the surge;
a broad, soft band of rufous pine needles;
a bar of sand; and shards of mica
glinting in the bright but tepid sun.

Here, really, we had only hard rain.
The cell I bought for the lamp
and kettles of water I drew remain
unused. All day we were restless, drowsy,
afraid, and finally, let down:
we didn't get to demonstrate our grit.

In the full, still pond the likeness
of golden birch leaves and the light they emit
shines exact. When the dog sees himself
his hackles rise. I stir away his trouble
with a stick.

A crow breaks in upon our satisfaction.
We look up to see it lift heavily
from its nest high in the hemlock, and the bough
equivocate in the peculiar light. It was
the author of *Walden*, wasn't it,
who made a sacrament of saying no.

After Working Long on One Thing

Through the screen door
I hear a hummingbird, inquiring
for nectar among the stalwart

hollyhocks—an erratic flying
ruby, asking for sweets among
the sticky-throated flowers.

The sky won't darken in the west
until ten. Where shall I turn
this light and tired mind?

Waking in January before Dawn

Something that sounded like the town
plow just went by: there must be snow.

What was it I fell asleep thinking
while the shutters strained on their hooks
in the wind, and the window frames
creaked as they do when it's terribly cold,
and getting colder fast? I pulled
the covers over my head.

Now through lace curtains I can see
the huge Wolf Moon going down,
and soon the sky will lighten, turning
first gray, then pink, then blue. . . .

How frightened I was as a child, waking
at Grandma's, though I saw
that the animal about to pounce
—a dreadful, vaguely organized beast—
was really the sewing machine.

Now the dresser reclaims visibility,
and yesterday's clothes cohere
humpbacked and headless on the chair.

Catching Frogs

I crouched beside the deepest pool,
and the smell of damp and moss
rose rich between my knees. Water-striders
creased the silver-black silky surface.
Rapt, I hardly breathed. Gnats
roiled in a shaft of sun.

Back again after supper I'd see
a nose poke up by the big flat stone
at the lip of the fall; then the humped
eyes and the slippery emerald head,
freckled brown. The buff membrane
pulsed under the jaw while
subtleties of timing played in my mind.

With a patience that came like grace
I waited. Mosquitoes moaned all
around. Better to wait. Better to reach
from behind. . . . It grew dark.

I came into the warm, bright room
where Father held aloft the evening
paper, and there was talk, and maybe
laughter, though I don't remember laughter.

In the Grove: The Poet at Ten

She lay on her back in the timothy
and gazed past the doddering
auburn heads of sumac.

A cloud—huge, calm,
and dignified—covered the sun
but did not, could not, put it out.

The light surged back again.

Nothing could rouse her then
from that joy so violent
it was hard to distinguish from pain.

The Pear

There is a moment in middle age
when you grow bored, angered
by your middling mind,
afraid.

That day the sun
burns hot and bright,
making you more desolate.

It happens subtly, as when a pear
spoils from the inside out,
and you may not be aware
until things have gone too far.

Christmas Away from Home

Her sickness brought me to Connecticut.
Mornings I walk the dog: that part of life
is intact. Who's painted, who's insulated
or put siding on, who's burned the lawn
with lime—that's the news on Ardmore Street.

The leaves of the neighbor's respectable
rhododendrons curl under in the cold.
He has backed the car
through the white nimbus of its exhaust
and disappeared for the day.

In the hiatus between mayors
the city has left leaves in the gutters,
and passing cars lift them in maelstroms.

We pass the house two doors down, the one
with the wildest lights in the neighborhood,
an establishment without irony.
All summer their *putto* empties a water jar,
their St. Francis feeds the birds.
Now it's angels, festoons, waist-high
candles, and swans pulling sleighs.

Two hundred miles north I'd let the dog
run among birches and the black shade of pines.
I miss the hills, the woods and stony
streams, where the swish of jacket sleeves

against my sides seems loud, and a crow
caws sleepily at dawn.

By now the streams must run under a skin
of ice, white air-bubbles passing erratically,
like blood cells through a vein. Soon the mail,
forwarded, will begin to reach me here.

Taking Down the Tree

"Give me some light!" cries Hamlet's
uncle midway through the murder
of Gonzago. "Light! Light!" cry scattering
courtesans. Here, as in Denmark,
it's dark at four, and even the moon
shines with only half a heart.

The ornaments go down into the box:
the silver spaniel, *My Darling*
on its collar, from Mother's childhood
in Illinois; the balsa jumping jack
my brother and I fought over,
pulling limb from limb. Mother
drew it together again with thread
while I watched, feeling depraved
at the age of ten.

With something more than caution
I handle them, and the lights, with their
tin star-shaped reflectors, brought along
from house to house, their pasteboard
toy suitcase increasingly flimsy.
Tick, tick, the desiccated needles drop.

By suppertime all that remains is the scent
of balsam fir. If it's darkness
we're having, let it be extravagant.

Dark Morning: Snow

It falls on the vole, nosing somewhere
through weeds, and on the open
eye of the pond. It makes the mail
come late.

The nuthatch spirals head first
down the tree.

I'm sleepy and benign in the dark.
There's nothing I want. . . .

Small Early Valentine

Wind plays the spy,
opens and closes doors,
looks behind shutters—
a succession of clatters. I
know perfectly well
where you are: in that
not-here-place you go to,
the antipodes. I have your note
with flights and phone numbers
for the different days. . . .
Dear one, I have made the bed
with the red sheets. Our
dog's the one who lay
on the deep pile of dung,
lifting his head and ears
when after twenty years
Odysseus approached him.

After the Dinner Party

A late-blooming burgundy hollyhock sways
across the kitchen window in a light breeze
as I draw a tumbler of well-water at the sink.
We're face to face, as in St. Paul's Epistles
or the later novels of Henry James.

The cold rains of autumn have begun.
Driving to Hanover I must have seen
a thousand frogs in the headlights
crossing the gleaming road. Like sheep urged
by a crouching dog they converged
and flowed, as they do every fall.
I couldn't help hitting some.

At dinner I laughed with the rest,
but in truth I prefer the sound
of pages turning, and coals shifting
abruptly in the stove. I left before ten
pleading a long drive home.

The smell of woodsmoke hung
over the small villages along the way.

I passed the huge cold gray stone
buildings left by the chaste Shakers.
Any window will still open with one finger.
Hands to work, and hearts to God. . . .

Why do people give dinner parties? Why did I
say I'd come? I suppose no one there was entirely
at ease. Again the flower leans this way:
you know it's impolite to stare. I'll put
out the light. . . . And there's an end to it.

Leaving Barbados

Just as the sun pitched summarily over
the edge of the world we arrived a week
ago. In the afterglow the sunburnt guests
finished their drinks by the pool.

That night we ate breadfruit, yams,
and flying fish in a dining room
with potted palms for walls. Beyond
the shoals a schooner, its rigging strung
with lights, passed by under moon and stars.
A scrawny kitten mewed beneath our chairs.

Letting go into sleep . . . the sound of crockery
being stacked in the kitchen, surf and wind.
A small dog barked inconclusively.

Next morning walking on the beach
I caught a whiff of marijuana mingled
with the reek of chicken coops, then
something like sterno, and fire.
Morning glories ramped over a tumbledown house.

Back at the hotel we settled in.
Levon came every day, wearing his T-shirt
that looked like the front of a tux—
which I saw one day drying on a porch
down the beach—and his heart-shaped
sunglasses, pushed back on his leonine
head so I could see his eyes, which were kind.
Cigarettes—funny cigarettes—he'd be your man.

Afternoons he surfed,
his beat-up board secured to his ankle
by a long strap. Perhaps that's how
the long scar came to be on his thigh.
The wind was up; the surf was loud and high.

Now our taxi strains uphill, its doors
ajog, then rushes down the narrow lane.
In the cut-over cane two egrets strut and peck.

Good-bye Barbados—good-bye water, hiss
and thunder; scented winds; clattering palms;
stupefying sun and rum; good-bye turquoise,
pink, copen, lavender, black and red.
Tonight another couple will sleep in our bed.

The Blue Bowl

Like primitives we buried the cat
with his bowl. Bare-handed
we scraped sand and gravel
back into the hole.
                            They fell with a hiss
and thud on his side,
on his long red fur, the white feathers
between his toes, and his
long, not to say aquiline, nose.

We stood and brushed each other off.
There are sorrows keener than these.

Silent the rest of the day, we worked,
ate, stared, and slept. It stormed
all night; now it clears, and a robin
burbles from a dripping bush
like the neighbor who means well
but always says the wrong thing.

The Letter

Bad news arrives in her distinctive hand.
The cancer has returned, this time
to his brain. Surgery impossible,
treatments underway. Hair loss, bouts
of sleeplessness and agitation at night,
exhaustion during the day . . .

I snap the blue leash onto the D-ring
of the dog's collar, and we cross
Route 4, then cut through the hayfield
to the pond road, where I let him run
along with my morbidity.

The trees have leafed out—only just—
and the air is misty with sap.
So green, so brightly, richly succulent,
this arbor over the road . . .
Sunlight penetrates in golden drops.

We come to the place where a neighbor
is taking timber from his land.
There's a smell of lacerated earth
and pine. Hardwood smells different.
His truck is gone.

Now you can see well up the slope,
see ledges of rock and ferns breaking forth
among the stumps and cast-aside limbs
and branches.

The place will heal itself in time, first
with weeds—goldenrod, cinquefoil, moth
mullein, then blackberries, sapling
pine, deciduous trees . . . but for now
the dog rolls, jovial, in the pungent
disturbance of wood and earth.

I summon him with a word, turn back,
and we go the long way home.

We Let the Boat Drift

I set out for the pond, crossing the ravine
where seedling pines start up like sparks
between the disused rails of the Boston and Maine.

The grass in the field would make a second crop
if early autumn rains hadn't washed
the goodness out. After the night's hard frost
it makes a brittle rustling as I walk.

The water is utterly still. Here and there
a black twig sticks up. It's five years today,
and even now I can't accept what cancer did
to him—not death so much as the annihilation
of the whole man, sense by sense, thought
by thought, hope by hope.

Once we talked about the life to come.
I took the Bible from the nightstand
and offered John 14: "I go to prepare
a place for you." "Fine. Good," he said.
"But what about Matthew? 'You, therefore,
must be perfect, as your heavenly Father
is perfect.'" And he wept.

My neighbor honks and waves driving by.
She counsels troubled students; keeps bees;
her goats follow her to the mailbox.

Last Sunday afternoon we went canoeing on the pond.
Something terrible at school had shaken her.
We talked quietly far from shore. The paddles

rested across our laps; glittering drops
fell randomly from their tips. The light
around us seemed alive. A loon—itinerant—
let us get quite close before it dove, coming up
after a long time, and well away from humankind.

Spring Changes

The autumnal drone of my neighbor
cutting wood across the pond
and the soundlessness of winter
give way to hammering. Must be
he's roofing, or building a shed
or fence. Some form of spring-induced
material advance.

Mother called early to say she's sold the house.
I'll fly out, help her sort and pack,
and give and throw away. One thing I'd like:
the yellow hand-painted pottery
vase that's crimped at the edge
like the crust of a pie—so gay, but
they almost never used it, who knows why?

A new young pair will paint and mow,
and fix the picket fence, wash windows face
to face in May, he outside on a ladder,
she inside on a chair, mouthing kisses
and "Be Careful!" through the glass.

Insomnia

The almost disturbing scent
of peonies presses through the screens,
and I know without looking how
those heavy white heads lean down
under the moon's light. A cricket chafes
and pauses, chafes and pauses,
as if distracted or preoccupied.

When I open my eyes to document
my sleeplessness by the clock, a point
of greenish light pulses near the ceiling.
A firefly . . . In childhood I ran out
at dusk, a jar in one hand, lid
pierced with airholes in the other,
getting soaked to the knees
in the long wet grass.

The light moves unsteadily, like someone
whose balance is uncertain after traveling
many hours, coming a long way.
Get up. Get up and let it out.

But I leave it hovering overhead, in case
it's my father, come back from the dead
to ask, "Why are you still awake? You can
put grass in their jar in the morning."

April Chores

When I take the chilly tools
from the shed's darkness, I come
out to a world made new
by heat and light.

The snake basks and dozes
on a large flat stone.
It reared and scolded me
for raking too close to its hole.

Like a mad red brain
the involute rhubarb leaf
thinks its way up
through loam.

The Clearing

The dog and I push through the ring
of dripping junipers
to enter the open space high on the hill
where I let him off the leash.

He vaults, snuffling, between tufts of moss;
twigs snap beneath his weight; he rolls
and rubs his jowls on the aromatic earth;
his pink tongue lolls.

I look for sticks of proper heft
to throw for him, while he sits, prim
and earnest in his love, if it is love.

All night a soaking rain, and now the hill
exhales relief, and the fragrance
of warm earth. . . .The sedges
have grown an inch since yesterday,
and ferns unfurled, and even if they try
the lilacs by the barn can't
keep from opening today.

I longed for spring's thousand tender greens,
and the white-throated sparrow's call
that borders on rudeness. Do you know—
since you went away
all I can do
is wait for you to come back to me.

Work

It has been light since four. In June
the birds find plenty to remark upon
at that hour. Pickup trucks, three men
to a cab, rush past burgeoning hay
and corn to summer constructions
up in town.
        Here, soon, the mowing, raking
and baling will begin. And I must tell
how, before the funeral all those years ago,
we lay down briefly on your grandparents'
bed, and that when you stood to put on
your jacket the change slipped
from your pants pocket.

Some dropped on the chenille
spread, and some hit the threadbare rug,
and one coin rolled onto the wide pine
floorboard under the dresser, hit
the molding, teetered and fell silent
like the rest. And oh, your sigh—
the sigh you sighed then. . . .

Private Beach

It is always the dispossessed—
someone driving a huge rusted Dodge
that's burning oil, and must cost
twenty-five dollars to fill.

Today before seven I saw, through
the morning fog, his car leave the road,
turning into the field. It must be
his day off, I thought, or he's out
of work and drinking, or getting stoned.
Or maybe as much as anything
he wanted to see
where the lane through the hay goes.

It goes to the bluff overlooking
the lake, where we've cleared
brush, swept the slippery oak
leaves from the path, and tried to destroy
the poison ivy that runs
over the scrubby, sandy knolls.

Sometimes in the evening I'll hear
gunshots or firecrackers. Later a car
needing a new muffler backs out
to the road, headlights withdrawing
from the lowest branches of the pines.

Next day I find beer cans, crushed;
sometimes a few fish too small
to bother cleaning and left
on the moss to die; or the leaking
latex trace of outdoor love. . . .
Once I found the canvas sling chairs
broken up and burned.

Whoever laid the fire gathered stones
to contain it, like a boy pursuing
a merit badge, who has a dream of work,
and proper reward for work.

At the Spanish Steps in Rome

Keats had come with his friend Severn
for the mild Roman winter. Afternoons
they walked to the Borghese Gardens
to see fine ladies, nannies with babies,
and handsome mounted officers,
whose horses moved sedately
along the broad and sandy paths.

But soon the illness kept him in.
Severn kept trying in that stoutly
cheerful English way: he rented a spinet,
hauled it three flights, turning it end
up on the landings, and played Haydn every day.

Love letters lay unopened in a chest.
"To see her hand writing would break my heart."

The poet's anger rose as his health sank.
He began to refer to his "posthumous
existence." One day while Severn and the porter
watched he flung, dish by dish, his catered
meal into the street.

Now the room where Keats died is a museum,
closed for several hours midday with the rest
of Rome. Waiting on the Steps in the wan
October sun I see the curator's pale,
exceptionally round face looking down.
Everything that was not burned that day
in accordance with the law is there.

Waiting

At the grocery store on a rainy July day
I pull in beside a family wagon:
Connecticut plates but no luggage—
summer people then, up for bright days
and cool nights, and local church fairs.
They may have been coming here for years.

Three little boys and a golden retriever
are steaming up the windows already smudged
by the dog's nose. The smallest boy
pitches himself repeatedly over the seat,
arms and legs flying, like some rubbery toy.
From time to time the dog woofs abstractedly.

Inside I look for their mother. And what
about their father—is he here too, or does he
come only on weekends and holidays
from Stamford, Farmington, or Darien?

There she is: of the right age, dressed
expensively, stiffly, carrying a straw
summer bag with a scrimshaw whale on the lid,
a hard little basket out of which she draws
a single large bill for the food. Clearly
this time she's come alone.

She will fill the cottage cupboards
and refrigerator, settle the boys
on the sleeping porch with one bunk bed

and one cot, and arbitrate the annual fight
over who gets to sleep on top.

And she will wait. Life is odd. . . .
I too am waiting, though if you asked
what for, I wouldn't know what to say.

Staying at Grandma's

Sometimes they left me for the day
while they went—what does it matter
where—away. I sat and watched her work
the dough, then turn the white shape
yellow in a buttered bowl.

A coleus, wrong to my eye because its leaves
were red, was rooting on the sill
in a glass filled with water and azure
marbles. I loved to see the sun
pass through the blue.

"You know," she'd say, turning
her straight and handsome back to me,
"that the body is the temple
of the Holy Ghost."

The Holy Ghost, the oh, oh . . . the *uh
oh,* I thought, studying the toe of my new shoe,
and glad she wasn't looking at me.

Soon I'd be back in school. No more mornings
at Grandma's side while she swept the walk
or shook the dust mop by the neck.

If she loved me why did she say that
two women would be grinding at the mill,
that God would come out of the clouds
when they were least expecting him,
choose one to be with him in heaven
and leave the other there alone?

Church Fair

Who knows what I might find
on tables under the maple trees—
perhaps a saucer in Aunt Lois's china pattern
to replace the one I broke
the summer I was thirteen, and visiting
for a week. Never in all these years
have I thought of it without
a warm surge of embarrassment.

I'll go through my own closets and cupboards
to find things for the auction.
I'll bake a peach pie for the food table,
and rolls for the supper,
Grandma Kenyon's recipe, which came down to me
along with her sturdy legs and brooding disposition.
"Mrs. Kenyon," the doctor used to tell her,
"you are simply killing yourself with work."
This she repeated often, with keen satisfaction.

She lived to be a hundred and three,
surviving all her children,
including the one so sickly at birth
that she had to carry him everywhere on a pillow
for the first four months. Father
suffered from a weak chest—bronchitis,
pneumonias, and pleurisy—and early on
books and music became his joy.

Surely these clothes are from another life—
not my own. I'll drop them off on the way
to town. I'm getting the peaches
today, so they'll be ripe by Saturday.

A Boy Goes into the World

My brother rode off on his bike
into the summer afternoon, but
Mother called me back
from the end of the sandy drive:
"It's different for girls."

He'd be gone for hours, come back
with things: a cocoon, gray-brown
and papery around a stick;
a puff ball, ripe, wrinkled,
and exuding spores; owl pellets—
bits of undigested bone and fur;
and pieces of moss that might
have made toupees for preposterous
green men, but went instead
into a wide-necked jar for a terrarium.

He mounted his plunder on poster
board, gluing and naming
each piece. He has long since
forgotten those days and things, but
I at last can claim them as my own.

The Three Susans

Ancient maples mingle over us, leaves
the color of pomegranates.
The days are warm with honey light,
but the last two nights have finished
every garden in the village.

The provident have left green tomatoes
to ripen on newspaper in the darkness of sheds.
The peppers were already in.
Now there will be no more corn.

I let myself through the wrought-iron gate
of the graveyard, and—meaning to exclude
the dog—I close it after me. But he runs
to the other end, and jumps the stone
wall overlooking Elbow Pond.

Here Samuel Smith lay down at last
with his three wives, all named Susan.
I had to see it for myself. They died
in their sixties, one outliving him.
So why do I feel indignant? He suffered.
Love and the Smiths' peculiar fame
"to nothingness do sink." And down the row
Sleepers are living up to their name.

The dog cocks his leg on a stone.
But animals do not mock, and the dead
may be glad to have life breaking in.

The sun drops low over the pond.
Long shadows move out from the stones,
and a chill rises from the moss,
prompt as a deacon. And at Keats's grave
in the Protestant cemetery in Rome
it is already night,
and wild cats are stalking in the moat.

Learning in the First Grade

"The cup is red. The drop of rain
is blue. The clam is brown."

So said the sheet of exercises—
purple mimeos, still heady
from the fluid in the rolling
silver drum. But the cup was

not red. It was white,
or had no color of its own.

Oh, but my mind was finical.
It put the teacher perpetually
in the wrong. Called on, however,
I said aloud: "The cup is red."

"But it's not," I thought,
like Galileo Galilei
muttering under his beard. . . .

At the Public Market Museum:
Charleston, South Carolina

A volunteer, a Daughter of the Confederacy,
receives my admission and points the way.
Here are gray jackets with holes in them,
red sashes with individual flourishes,
things soft as flesh. Someone sewed
the gold silk cord onto that gray sleeve
as if embellishments
could keep a man alive.

I have been reading *War and Peace,*
and so the particulars of combat
are on my mind—the shouts and groans
of men and boys, and the horses' cries
as they fall, astonished at what
has happened to them.
                              Blood on leaves,
blood on grass, on snow; extravagant
beauty of red. Smoke, dust of disturbed
earth; parch and burn.

Who would choose this for himself?
And yet the terrible machinery
waited in place. With psalters
in their breast pockets, and gloves
knitted by their sisters and sweethearts,
the men in gray hurled themselves
out of the trenches, and rushed against
blue. It was what both sides
agreed to do.

Lines for Akhmatova

The night train from Moscow, beginning to slow,
pulled closer to your sleeping city.
A sound like tiny bells in cold air . . . Then
the attendant appeared with glasses of strong tea.
"Wake up, ladies! This is Leningrad."

The narrow canals gleam black and still
under ornate street lamps, and in the parks
golden leaves lie on the sandy paths
and wooden benches. By light of day
old women dressed in black sweep them away
with birch stick brooms.

Your work, your amorous life, your scholarship—
everything happened here, where the Party
silenced you for twenty-five years
for writing about love—a middle-class activity.

Husband and son, lovers, dear companions
were imprisoned or killed, emigrated or died.
You turned still further inward,
imperturbable as a lion-gate, and lived on
stubbornly, learning Dante by heart.

In the end you outlived the genocidal
Georgian with his mustache thick as a snake.
And in triumph, an old woman, you wrote:
I can't tell if the day is ending, or the world,
or if the secret of secrets is within me again.

Heavy Summer Rain

The grasses in the field have toppled,
and in places it seems that a large, now
absent, animal must have passed the night.
The hay will right itself if the day

turns dry. I miss you steadily, painfully.
None of your blustering entrances
or exits, doors swinging wildly
on their hinges, or your huge unconscious
sighs when you read something sad,
like Henry Adams's letters from Japan,
where he traveled after Clover died.

Everything blooming bows down in the rain:
white irises, red peonies; and the poppies
with their black and secret centers
lie shattered on the lawn.

September Garden Party

We sit with friends at the round
glass table. The talk is clever;
everyone rises to it. Bees
come to the spiral pear peelings
on your plate.
From my lap or your hand
the spice of our morning's privacy
comes drifting up. Fall sun
passes through the wine.

While We Were Arguing

The first snow fell—or should I say
it flew slantwise, so it seemed
to be the house
that moved so heedlessly through space.

Tears splashed and beaded on your sweater.
Then for long moments you did not speak.
No pleasure in the cups of tea I made
distractedly at four.

The sky grew dark. I heard the paper come
and went out. The moon looked down
between disintegrating clouds. I said
aloud: "You see, we have done harm."

Dry Winter

So little snow that the grass in the field
like a terrible thought
has never entirely disappeared. . . .

On the Aisle

Leaving Maui—orchids on our plates,
whales seen from the balcony at cocktail hour,
and Mai Tais bristling with fruit—
we climb through thirty-two thousand feet
with retired schoolteachers, widows on tours,
and honeymooners. The man and woman next to me,
young, large, bronze, and prosperous,
look long without fear or shame
into each other's faces.

Anxious, I am grateful for rum, my last
island draught, and the circulation
of the blood, and I begin Gogol's story
about a painter whose love of luxury
destroys his art. People pull down
their window shades, shutting out the sun,
and a movie called *Clue* comes on.
I continue to read in my pillar of light
like a village schoolmistress, while
from the dark on my right comes
the sound of kissing. It would be a lie
to say I didn't sneak a look.

On the slow approach to rainy San Francisco
I find I had things figured wrong:
"Don't worry, OK? He's still out of town."
I stop speculating about their occupations
and combined income. They fall silent again.

We hit the runway and bounce three times.
After what seems too long the nose comes down;

I feel the brakes go on. Their grief is real
when my seatmates part at the gate. He has
a close connection to Tucson,
and runs for it.

At the Winter Solstice

The pines look black in the half-
light of dawn. Stillness . . .
While we slept an inch of new snow
simplified the field. Today of all days
the sun will shine no more
than is strictly necessary.

At the village church last night
the boys—shepherds and wisemen—
pressed close to the manger in obedience,
wishing only for time to pass;
but the girl dressed as Mary trembled
as she leaned over the pungent hay,
and like the mother of Christ
wondered why she had been chosen.

After the pageant, a ruckus of cards,
presents, and homemade Christmas sweets.
A few of us stayed to clear the bright
scraps and ribbons from the pews,
and lift the pulpit back in place.

When I opened the hundred-year-old Bible
to Luke's account of the Epiphany
black dust from the binding rubbed off
on my hands, and on the altar cloth.

The Guest

I had opened the draft on the stove
and my head was tending downward when
a portly housefly dropped on the page
in front of me. Confused by the woodstove's
heat, the fly, waking ill-tempered, lay
on its back, flailing its legs and wings.

Then it lurched into the paper clips.
The morning passed, and I forgot about
my guest, except when the buzz rose
and quieted, rose and quieted—tires
spinning on ice, chain saw far away,
someone carrying on alone. . . .

Father and Son

August. My neighbor started cutting wood
on cool Sabbath afternoons, the blue
plume of the saw's exhaust wavering over
his head. At first I didn't mind the noise
but it came to seem like a species of pain.

From time to time he let the saw idle,
stepping back from the logs and aromatic
dust, while his son kicked the billets
down the sloping drive toward the shed.
In the lull they sometimes talked.

His back ached unrelentingly, he assumed
from all the stooping. Sundays that fall
they bent over the pile of beech and maple,
intent on getting wood for winter, the last,
as it happened, of their life together.

Three Crows

Three crows fly across a gun-metal
sky. Turgenev, in love for forty years
with Pauline Viardot . . .

Paris, Baden, wherever she and Louis lived
the writer followed, writing books
in which love invariably goes awry.
The men hunted small game companionably.

Spring rain, relentless as obsession:
the mountain streams run swift and full.
The red tassels of blossoming maples
hang bright against wet black bark.

"I lived," he said, "all my life
on the edge of another's nest."

Spring Snow

A thoughtful snow comes falling . . .
seems to hang in the air before
concluding that it must fall
here. Huge aggregate flakes

alight on the muddy ruts
of March, and the standing
water that thaws by day
and freezes by night.

Venus is content to shine unseen
this evening, having risen serene
above springs, and false springs.
But I, restless after supper, pace

the long porch while the snow falls,
dodging the clothesline I won't
use until peonies send up red,
plump, irrepressible spears.

Ice Out

As late as yesterday ice preoccupied
the pond—dark, half-melted, waterlogged.
Then it sank in the night, one piece,
taking winter with it. And afterward
everything seems simple and good.

All afternoon I lifted oak leaves
from the flowerbeds, and greeted
like friends the green-white crowns
of perennials. They have the tender,
unnerving beauty of a baby's head.

How I hated to come in! I've left
the windows open to hear the peepers'
wildly disproportionate cries.
Dinner is over, no one stirs. The dog
sighs, sneezes, and closes his eyes.

Going Away

Like Varya in *The Cherry Orchard*
I keep the keys, and go around locking
the new deadbolts, meant to ward off
antique thieves: loud, satisfying clicks.

When I am walking down some broad, linden-
lined boulevard where people pass
whole afternoons at tables in dappled
shade, and where the cries of news vendors

mean nothing to me, I'll be glad
that I've overwatered all the plants,
stopped the mail, and wound the clock
to tick and chime as if I were at home.

The dog has understood the melancholy
meaning of open satchels and has hurled
himself down by the door, hoping not to be
left in the silent house, like Firs. . . .

Now Where?

It wakes when I wake, walks
when I walk, turns back when I
turn back, beating me to the door.

It spoils my food and steals
my sleep, and mocks me, saying,
"Where is your God now?"

And so, like a widow, I lie down
after supper. If I lie down
or sit up it's all the same:

the days and nights bear me along.
To strangers I must seem
alive. Spring comes, summer;

cool clear weather; heat, rain. . . .

Letter to Alice

Twilight. A few bats loop out of the barn,
dip and veer, feeding on flies and midges
in humid air. Before the storm
I top-dressed the perennials with manure,
ashes from the stove, and bonemeal.
The rain soaking through the black
and white makes a mad, elemental tea.

I bought the bonemeal up in New London,
where the streets are crowded for the summer
with stately Episcopalians—and I've noticed
that it hardly smells.

We made less than usual on the Church Fair supper,
held this year in the Blazing Star Grange,
because of rain. Down in the valley
we're land-rich but cash-poor, shorter,
stouter, and lower-church.

By now the blackflies are biting more out of habit
than desire, and graduation night is over.
I've picked up all the beer cans
from the pond road to the bridge.

The fully open peonies seem overcome by rain
and carnality. I should stake them: white
doubles with a raspberry fleck
at the heart, blooming without restraint

in the moist summer night. I planted them
just last fall, and this is a good showing
for their first year. More flowers, more art.

Write!

After an Illness, Walking the Dog

Wet things smell stronger,
and I suppose his main regret is that
he can sniff just one at a time.
In a frenzy of delight
he runs way up the sandy road—
scored by freshets after five days
of rain. Every pebble gleams, every leaf.

When I whistle he halts abruptly
and steps in a circle,
swings his extravagant tail.
Then he rolls and rubs his muzzle
in a particular place, while the drizzle
falls without cease, and Queen Anne's lace
and goldenrod bend low.

The top of the logging road stands open
and bright. Another day, before
hunting starts, we'll see how far it goes,
leaving word first at home.
The footing is ambiguous.

Soaked and muddy, the dog drops,
panting, and looks up with what amounts
to a grin. It's so good to be uphill with him,
nicely winded, and looking down on the pond.

A sound commences in my left ear
like the sound of the sea in a shell;
a downward vertiginous drag comes with it.

Time to head home. I wait
until we're nearly out to the main road
to put him back on the leash, and he
—the designated optimist—
imagines to the end that he is free.

Wash Day

How it rained while you slept! Wakeful,
I wandered around feeling the sills,
followed closely by the dog and cat.
We conferred, and left a few windows
open a crack.
            Now the morning is clear
and bright, the wooden clothespins
swollen after the wet night.

 The monkshood has slipped its stakes
and the blue cloaks drag in the mud.
Even the daisies—good-hearted
simpletons—seem cast down.

We have reached and passed the zenith.
The irises, poppies, and peonies, and the old
shrub roses with their romantic names
and profound attars have gone by
like young men and women of promise
who end up living indifferent lives.

How is it that every object in this basket
got to be inside out? There must be
a trickster in the hamper, a backward,
unclean spirit.
            The clothes—the thicker
things—may not get dry by dusk.
The days are getting shorter. . . .
You'll laugh, but I feel it—
some power has gone from the sun.

Geranium

How many years did I lug it, pale and leggy,
onto the porch for the summer? There its stems
turned thick, its leaves curly and dark,
and it bloomed almost immediately.

Before first frost I'd bring it back inside
where it yellowed like the soles of the feet
of someone very old. Its flowers fell apart.

One spring I cut back all but one shoot,
and that I tied against a bamboo stake
to make a long straight stem.
Then I pinched out the new growth repeatedly
until I had a full, round ball on a stick,
like topiary at Versailles. It pleased me well;
its flowers were salmon pink.

I fed it fish emulsion, bonemeal, wood
ashes; mulched it with cocoa pod hulls,
gave it a Tuscan terra-cotta pot.
It was my nightingale, my goose, my golden
child. We drank from the same cup.

After the night's downpour I find the top
snapped off, lying on the ground like a rack
of antlers. Not even wilted yet—I've come
upon the fresh disaster. . . . Like Beethoven's
head its head had grown too large.

Cultural Exchange

A postcard arrives from a friend
visiting the Great Wall of China.
"Life couldn't be better," says M.

I was there once, in March. Unkind wind
bore down from the north. Mongolia . . .
how steep it is! In places even presidents
are forced to drop down on all fours.

On the way back to Beijing
our embassy car rushed wildly
through a succession of hamlets, forcing
bicycles off the road, dooryard
fowl to flap and fluster, and from
grandmother, bundled in her blue jacket
to take the pale sun, such a look!

Tired? Tired was not the word.
Getting sleepy in the warm car
I considered the Wall, the scale
of enterprise. A lock of hair had fallen
across my eyes. At last my brain
convinced my hand to move it.

That night I was honored by a banquet
in a room so cold I could see my breath.

Homesick

My clothes and hair smell stale,
and more than once I have slept in my coat
on trains that crashed past isolated stations
where magnolias bloom all night
beside dusty platform benches.

Twice I bought dried fish rolled
in cellophane, thinking it was pastry.

Leaving the pebbled Buddhist garden
such a dreadful languor overtook me;
I could hardly step over the threshold.
The monks were eating bean curd
fixed eleven different ways
and drinking bowls of frothy bitter green tea.

Oh my bed, and the dear dust under it!
Bath towels that don't smell like miso soup;
my own little dog, one ear up
and one ear down, and a speaker of English;
the teller at the village bank
who never asks to see my passport . . .

"Yes," I'll say, "we had a wonderful time.
We slept on pillows filled with cottonseed,
ate cuttlefish, dried squid, and black bean
paste, and drank pink laurel wine."

Summer: 6:00 A.M.

From the shadowy upstairs bedroom
of my mother-in-law's house in Hamden
I hear the neighbors' children waking.

"Ahhhhhhhh," says the infant, not
unhappily. "Yes, yes, yes, yes, yes!"
replies the toddler to his mother,
who must have forbidden something.
It is hot already at this hour
and the houses are wholly open.
If she is cross with the child
anyone with ears will hear.

The slap of sprinkler water
hitting the sidewalk and street,
and the husband's deliberate footfalls
receding down the drive . . .

His Japanese sedan matches the house.
Beige, brown . . . Yesterday he washed it,
his arm thrust deep into something
that looked like a sheepskin oven mitt.

His wife had put the babies
in the shallow plastic wading
pool, and she took snapshots, trying
repeatedly to get both boys to look.
The older one's wail rose
and matched the pitch of the cicada
in a nearby tree. Why

is the sound of a spoon on a plate
next door a thing so desolate?
I think of the woman pouring a glass of juice
for the three-year-old, and watching him
spill it, knowing he *must* spill it,
seeing the ineluctable downward course
of the orange-pink liquid, the puddle
swell on the kitchen
floor beside the child's shoe.

Walking Notes: Hamden, Connecticut

Wearing only her nightdress
with a white sweater thrown over her shoulders,
a woman stands at the curb, watching
with a look of love and patience
as her aged poodle snuffles at a candy wrapper.
I see her as her husband of forty years
sees her: hair tied back by a broad, pink
ribbon, eyes swollen with sleep.

My daily walk takes me past a house
where roses scramble lustily
up the trellises, a Dorothy Perkins
and a climbing Peace.

The house where two dentists, Dr. Charles Molloy
and Dr. Everett Condon, drill and pack . . .
The boys in the neighborhood call Dr. Condon
Dr. Condom. They know all about such things
though their parents have told them little
about sex, leaving that to luck, or the lack
of it, or lurid films on hygiene in gym class.

The girl next door, a real beauty, her long black
curls drawn up with combs like someone in Turgenev,
waters the lawn, not thoroughly. Her father
is about to be indicted for racketeering.
For a long time they didn't mow. The wind
carried weed seeds into the neighbors' yards.
Everyone was irate. . . .Then suddenly
he mowed, and now she waters listlessly.

Last Days

Over the orchard a truly black cloud appeared.
Then horizontal rain began, and apples fell
before their time. Leaves blew
in phalanxes along the ground. Doors
opened and closed of their own accord. The lights
went out, but then thought better of it.

So I sat with her in a room made small
by the paraphernalia of the mortally ill.
Among ranks of brown bottles from the pharmacy
a hymnbook lay open on the chest of drawers:
"Safely Through Another Week." Indifferent,
a housefly lit on her blue-white brow.

Looking at Stars

The God of curved space, the dry
God, is not going to help us, but the son
whose blood spattered
the hem of his mother's robe.

At the Dime Store

Since I saw him last his teeth have gone.
The gaps draw my eyes, and like Saint
Paul I give way: that very thing I would
not do, I do. He notices, abashed.

Most of one summer he was around, coming
by seven each morning with his rascally look
to build a new wing and replace the old
north sill. Sometimes he'd disappear for a day
or a week. There was trouble at home
and on his lunch hour he'd call—just over
the town line and so long distance—
thinking we couldn't hear or wouldn't
care. This was years ago.

When I encounter him again in the aisles
we both grin shyly. His boy, tall suddenly,
and bulky, not built like his father at all,
joins him at the checkout.
They've got an aquarium in their cart.

At last the job was finished. All but
taking up the piles of extra shingles,
sawhorses, and lumber from the back
yard. Weeks passed. I called. Yes,
his wife assured me, he'd be coming by.

And finally one day he did
while I was up in town having a filling

replaced. When I got home, shaky
and feeling mussed, I saw that everything
of substance was gone, leaving only
white rectangular spaces on the lawn.

Let Evening Come

Let the light of late afternoon
shine through chinks in the barn, moving
up the bales as the sun moves down.

Let the cricket take up chafing
as a woman takes up her needles
and her yarn. Let evening come.

Let dew collect on the hoe abandoned
in long grass. Let the stars appear
and the moon disclose her silver horn.

Let the fox go back to its sandy den.
Let the wind die down. Let the shed
go black inside. Let evening come.

To the bottle in the ditch, to the scoop
in the oats, to air in the lung
let evening come.

Let it come, as it will, and don't
be afraid. God does not leave us
comfortless, so let evening come.

With the Dog at Sunrise

Although we always come this way
I never noticed before that the poplars
growing along the ravine
shine pink in the light of winter dawn.

What am I going to say
in my letter to Sarah—a widow
at thirty-one, alone in the violence
of her grief, sleepless,
and utterly cast down?

I look at the lithe, pink trees more carefully,
remembering Stephen, the photographer.
With the hunger of two I take them in.
Perhaps I can tell her that.

The dog furrows his brow while pissing long
and thoughtfully against an ancient hemlock.
The snow turns the saffron of a monk's robe
and acrid steam ascends.

Searching for God is the first thing and the last,
but in between such trouble, and such pain.

Far up in the woods where no one goes
deer take their ease under the great
pines, nose to steaming nose. . . .

Constance

(1993)

— Perkins, ever for Perkins

From Psalm 139
"O Lord, thou hast searched me . . ."

Whither shall I go from thy spirit?
   or whither shall I flee from thy presence?

If I ascend up into heaven, thou art there:
   if I make my bed in hell, behold, thou art there.

If I take the wings of the morning,
   and dwell in the uttermost parts of the sea;

Even there shall thy hand lead me,
   and thy right hand shall hold me.

If I say, Surely the darkness shall cover me;
   even the night shall be light about me.

Yea, the darkness hideth not from thee;
   but the night shineth as the day:
   the darkness and the light are both alike to thee. . . .

I

The Progress of a Beating Heart

August Rain, after Haying

Through sere trees and beheaded
grasses the slow rain falls.
Hay fills the barn; only the rake
and one empty wagon are left
in the field. In the ditches
goldenrod bends to the ground.

Even at noon the house is dark.
In my room under the eaves
I hear the steady benevolence
of water washing dust
raised by the haying
from porch and car and garden
chair. We are shorn
and purified, as if tonsured.

The grass resolves to grow again,
receiving the rain to that end,
but my disordered soul thirsts
after something it cannot name.

The Stroller

1949

It was copen blue, strong and bright,
and the metal back looked like caning
on a chair. The peanut-shaped tray
had a bar with sliding beads:
red, yellow, blue, green, white.
It was hard for Mother to push the stroller
on the sandy shoulders of the road.

Sitting in the stroller
in the driveway of the new house
on a morning in early spring, trees
leafing out, I could hear cows
lowing in their stalls across the road,
and see geese hissing and flapping
at a sheep that wandered too close
to the goslings. From the stroller I surveyed
my new domain like a dowager queen.
When something pleased me I kicked
my feet and spun the bright beads.
Spittle dropped from my lower lip
like a spider plunging on its filament.

1991

Mother is moving; we're sorting
through fifty years' accumulations—
a portfolio of Father's drawings
from his brief career in Architecture
School, exercises in light and shadow,
vanishing point; renderings of acanthus

cornices, gargoyles. . . .Then I come upon
a drawing of my stroller, precisely to scale,
just as I remember it.

And here is a self-portrait, looser,
where he wears the T-shirt whose stripes
I know were red and white
although the drawing is pencil.
Beside Father, who sits in a blue chair
that I remember, by a bookcase I remember,
under a lamp I remember, is the empty stroller.

1951

He was forty-seven, a musician
who took other jobs to get by,
a dreamer, a reader, a would-be farmer
with weak lungs from many pneumonias
and from playing cocktail piano
late in smoky bars. On weekend mornings
we crept around so he could sleep until ten.

When he came home from his day-job
at the bookstore, I untied his shoes.
I waited all day to untie them,
wanting no other happiness. I was four.
He never went to town without a suit
and tie, a linen handkerchief
in his pocket, and his shoes
were good leather, the laces themselves
leather. I loved the rich pungency
of his brown, well-shined, warm shoes.

1959

Mother took in sewing.
One by one Ann Arbor's bridge club
ladies found her. They pulled into our drive
in their Thunderbirds and Cadillacs
as I peered down between muslin curtains
from my room. I lay back on the bed, thinking
of nothing in particular, until they went
away. When I came downstairs the scent
of cigarettes and perfume persisted in the air.

One of them I liked. She took
her two dachshunds everywhere
on a bifurcated leash; they hopped comically
up the porch steps and into our house.
She was Italian, from Modena, displaced,
living in Ann Arbor as the wife
of a Chrysler executive. She never wore
anything but beige or gray knits.
She was six feet tall and not ashamed of it,
with long, loose red hair held back
by tortoiseshell combs. She left cigarette
butts in the ashtray with bright red
striated crescents on them.

She was different from the others,
attached to my mother in the way
European women are attached
to their dressmakers and hairdressers.
When she traveled abroad

she brought back classical recordings
and perfume. I thought I would not mind
being like Marcella, though I recognized
that she was lonely. Her husband traveled
frequently, and she had a son
living in Florence who never came "home."
His enterprises were obscure. . . .
Marcella had her dogs, her solitude,
her elegance—at once sedate and slightly
wild—and, it seemed, a new car every time
the old one got dirty, a luxury
to which she seemed oblivious.

1991

Disturbed but full of purpose, we push
Father's indifferent drawings into the trash.
Mother saves the self-portrait and the acanthus
cornice. I save only the rendering
of the stroller, done on tracing paper, diaphanous.

Looking at it
is like looking into a mirror
and seeing your own eyes and someone else's
eyes as well, strange to you
but benign, curious, come
to interrogate your wounds, the progress
of your beating heart.

The Argument

On the way to the village store
I drive through a downdraft
from the neighbor's chimney.
Woodsmoke tumbles from the eaves
backlit by sun, reminding me
of the fire and sulfur of Grandmother's
vengeful God, the one who disapproves
of jeans and shorts for girls,
dancing, strong waters, and adultery.

A moment later the smoke enters
the car, although the windows are tight,
insinuating that I might, like Judas,
and the foolish virgins, and the rich
young man, have been made for unquenchable
fire. God will need something to burn
if the fire is to be unquenchable.

"All things work together for the good
for those who love God," she said
to comfort me at Uncle Hazen's funeral,
where Father held me up to see
the maroon gladiolus that trembled
as we approached the bier, the elaborate
shirred satin, brass fittings, anything,

oh, anything but Uncle's squelched
and made-up face.
"No! NO! How is it good to be dead?"

I cried afterward, wild-eyed and flushed.
"God's ways are not our ways,"
she said then out of pity
and the wish to forestall the argument.

Biscuit

The dog has cleaned his bowl
and his reward is a biscuit,
which I put in his mouth
like a priest offering the host.

I can't bear that trusting face!
He asks for bread, expects
bread, and I in my power
might have given him a stone.

Not Writing

A wasp rises to its papery
nest under the eaves
where it daubs

at the gray shape,
but seems unable
to enter its own house.

Windfalls

The storm is moving on, and as the wind
rises, the oaks and pines let go
of all the snow on their branches,
an abrupt change of heart,
and the air turns utterly white.

Woooh, says the wind, and I stop
where I am, put out my arms
and look upward, allowing
myself to disappear. It is good
to be here, and not here. . . .

I see fresh cloven prints
under the apple tree, where deer come
nosing for windfalls. They must be
near me now, and having stopped
when I stopped, begin to move again.

II

Tell me how to bear myself . . .

Adrienne Rich

Having It Out with Melancholy

> If many remedies are prescribed for an illness,
> you may be certain that the illness has no cure.
>
> A. P. Chekhov
> *The Cherry Orchard*

1 *From the Nursery*

When I was born, you waited
behind a pile of linen in the nursery,
and when we were alone, you lay down
on top of me, pressing
the bile of desolation into every pore.

And from that day on
everything under the sun and moon
made me sad—even the yellow
wooden beads that slid and spun
along a spindle on my crib.

You taught me to exist without gratitude.
You ruined my manners toward God:
"We're here simply to wait for death;
the pleasures of earth are overrated."

I only appeared to belong to my mother,
to live among blocks and cotton undershirts
with snaps; among red tin lunch boxes
and report cards in ugly brown slipcases.
I was already yours—the anti-urge,
the mutilator of souls.

2 Bottles

Elavil, Ludiomil, Doxepin,
Norpramin, Prozac, Lithium, Xanax,
Wellbutrin, Parnate, Nardil, Zoloft.
The coated ones smell sweet or have
no smell; the powdery ones smell
like the chemistry lab at school
that made me hold my breath.

3 Suggestion from a Friend

You wouldn't be so depressed
if you really believed in God.

4 Often

Often I go to bed as soon after dinner
as seems adult
(I mean I try to wait for dark)
in order to push away
from the massive pain in sleep's
frail wicker coracle.

5 Once There Was Light

Once, in my early thirties, I saw
that I was a speck of light in the great
river of light that undulates through time.

I was floating with the whole
human family. We were all colors—those
who are living now, those who have died,
those who are not yet born. For a few

moments I floated, completely calm,
and I no longer hated having to exist.

Like a crow who smells hot blood
you came flying to pull me out
of the glowing stream.
"I'll hold you up. I never let my dear
ones drown!" After that, I wept for days.

6 In and Out

The dog searches until he finds me
upstairs, lies down with a clatter
of elbows, puts his head on my foot.

Sometimes the sound of his breathing
saves my life—in and out, in
and out; a pause, a long sigh. . . .

7 Pardon

A piece of burned meat
wears my clothes, speaks
in my voice, dispatches obligations
haltingly, or not at all.
It is tired of trying

to be stouthearted, tired
beyond measure.

We move on to the monoamine
oxidase inhibitors. Day and night
I feel as if I had drunk six cups
of coffee, but the pain stops
abruptly. With the wonder
and bitterness of someone pardoned
for a crime she did not commit
I come back to marriage and friends,
to pink-fringed hollyhocks; come back
to my desk, books, and chair.

8 Credo

Pharmaceutical wonders are at work
but I believe only in this moment
of well-being. Unholy ghost,
you are certain to come again.

Coarse, mean, you'll put your feet
on the coffee table, lean back,
and turn me into someone who can't
take the trouble to speak; someone
who can't sleep, or who does nothing
but sleep; can't read, or call
for an appointment for help.

There is nothing I can do
against your coming.
When I awake, I am still with thee.

9 Wood Thrush

High on Nardil and June light
I wake at four,
waiting greedily for the first
notes of the wood thrush. Easeful air
presses through the screen
with the wild, complex song
of the bird, and I am overcome

by ordinary contentment.
What hurt me so terribly
all my life until this moment?
How I love the small, swiftly
beating heart of the bird
singing in the great maples;
its bright, unequivocal eye.

Litter

I poured the unused coffee grounds
from the paper filter back
into the can. I was too rattled
to spoon the dry Cream of Wheat
back into the packet, so I threw it away.

The neighbor who rushed over
had straightened the bedcovers.
The violets were dry; I watered them.

I picked up the blue plastic syringe
tips, strips of white tape,
and the backing from bandages
that the EMTs had dropped in haste.

Now curtains lift and fall
in windows I've never before seen open.

Chrysanthemums

The doctor averted his eyes
while the diagnosis fell on us,
as though the picture of the girl
hiding from her dog
had suddenly fallen off the wall.
We were speechless all the way home.
The light seemed strange.

A weekend of fear and purging. . . .
Determined to work, he packed his
Dictaphone, a stack of letters,
and a roll of stamps. At last the day
of scalpels, blood, and gauze arrived.

Eyes closed, I lay on his tightly made
bed, waiting. From the hallway I heard
an old man, whose nurse was helping him
to walk: "That Howard Johnson's. It's
nothing but the same thing over and over
again."
   "That's right. It's nothing special."

Late in the afternoon, when slanting
sun betrayed a wad of dust under the bed-
side stand, I heard the sound of casters
and footsteps slowing down.
The attendants asked me to leave the room
while they moved him onto the bed,
and the door remained closed a long time.

Evening came. . . .
While he dozed, fitfully, still stupefied
by anesthetics, I tried to read,
my feet propped on the rails of the bed.
Odette's chrysanthemums
were revealed to me, ranks of them
in the house where Swann, jealousy
constricting his heart, made late-night calls.

And while I read, pausing again
and again to look at him, the smell
of chrysanthemums sent by friends
wavered from the sill, mixing
with the smells of drastic occasions
and disinfected sheets.

He was too out of it
to press the bolus for medication.
Every eight minutes, when he could have
more, I pressed it, and morphine dripped
from the vial in the locked box
into his arm. I made a hive
of eight-minute cells
where he could sleep without pain,
or beyond caring about pain.

Over days the IVs came out,
and freedom came back to him—
walking, shaving, sitting in a chair.
The most ordinary gestures seemed

cause for celebration.
Hazy with analgesics, he read
the *Boston Globe,* and began to talk
on the telephone.

Once the staples were out,
and we had the discharge papers
in hand, I brought him home, numbed up
for the trip. He dozed in the car,
woke, and looked with astonishment
at the hills, gold and quince
under October sun, a sight so
overwhelming that we began to cry,
he first, and then I.

Climb

From the porch of our house we can see
Mt. Kearsarge, the huge, black-green
presence that tells us where we are,
and what the weather is going to be.
By night we see the red beacon
on the fire warden's tower, by day
the tower itself, minute with distance.

Yesterday I climbed it with a friend
just home from the hospital.
She'd thought the second coming was at hand,
and found herself in a private
room, tastefully appointed, on a ward
she couldn't leave.

We talked and panted, stopped to look
at the undersides of sage and pink
opalescent mushrooms. Our shirts
were wet with effort.

At last, we sprawled on the gray granite
ledges, with veins and blotches of pink
and silver-green lichen, growing like fur.
We looked for our houses; shreds of clouds
floated between our heads; and we saw from above
the muscular shoulders of a patient hawk.

Back

We try a new drug, a new combination
of drugs, and suddenly
I fall into my life again

like a vole picked up by a storm
then dropped three valleys
and two mountains away from home.

I can find my way back. I know
I will recognize the store
where I used to buy milk and gas.

I remember the house and barn,
the rake, the blue cups and plates,
the Russian novels I loved so much,

and the black silk nightgown
that he once thrust
into the toe of my Christmas stocking.

Moving the Frame

Impudent spring has come
since your chest rose and fell
for the last time, bringing
the push and ooze of budding peonies,
with ants crawling over them
exuberantly.

I have framed the picture
from your obituary. It must have been
taken on a hot graduation day:
You're wearing your academic robes
—how splendid they were—
and your hair and beard are curly
with sweat. The tassel sways. . . .
No matter how I move your face
around my desk,
your eyes don't meet my eyes.

There was one hard night
while your breath became shallower
and shallower, and then
you were gone from us. A person
simply vanishes! I came home
and fell deeply asleep for a long
time, but I woke up again.

Fear of Death Awakens Me

. . . or it's a cloud-shadow passing over Tuckerman Ravine, darkening the warm ledges and alpine vegetation, then moving on. Sunlight reasserts itself, and that dark, moving lane is like something that never happened, something misremembered, dreamed in anxious sleep.

Or it's like swimming unexpectedly into cold water in a spring-fed pond. Fear locates in my chest, instant and profound, and I speed up my stroke, or turn back the way I came, hoping to avoid more cold.

III

Peonies at Dusk

Winter Lambs

All night snow came upon us
with unwavering intent—
small flakes not meandering
but driving thickly down. We woke
to see the yard, the car and road
heaped unrecognizably.

The neighbors' ewes are lambing
in this stormy weather. Three
lambs born yesterday, three more
expected . . .
          Felix the ram looked
proprietary in his separate pen
while fatherhood accrued to him.
The panting ewes regarded me
with yellow-green, small-
pupiled eyes.

I have a friend who is pregnant—
plans gone awry—and not altogether
pleased. I don't say she should
be pleased. We are creation's
property, its particles, its clay
as we fall into this life,
agree or disagree.

Not Here

Searching for pillowcases trimmed
with lace that my mother-in-law
once made, I open the chest of drawers
upstairs to find that mice
have chewed the blue and white linen
dishtowels to make their nest,
and bedded themselves
among embroidered dresser scarves
and fingertip towels.

Tufts of fibers, droppings like black
caraway seeds, and the stains of birth
and afterbirth give off the strong
unforgettable attar of mouse
that permeates an old farmhouse
on humid summer days.

A couple of hickory nuts
roll around as I lift out
the linens, while a hail of black
sunflower shells
falls on the pillowcases,
yellow with age, but intact.
I'll bleach them and hang them in the sun
to dry. There's almost no one left
who knows how to crochet lace. . . .

The bright-eyed squatters are not here.
They've scuttled out to the fields
for summer, as they scuttled in
for winter—along the wall, from chair

to skirted chair, making themselves
flat and scarce while the cat
dozed with her paws in the air,
and we read the mail
or evening paper, unaware.

Coats

I saw him leaving the hospital
with a woman's coat over his arm.
Clearly she would not need it.
The sunglasses he wore could not
conceal his wet face, his bafflement.

As if in mockery the day was fair,
and the air mild for December. All the same
he had zipped his own coat and tied
the hood under his chin, preparing
for irremediable cold.

In Memory of Jack

Once, coming down the long hill
into Andover on an autumn night
just before deer season, I stopped
the car abruptly to avoid a doe.

She stood, head down, perhaps twenty
feet away, her legs splayed
as if she meant to stand her ground.

For a long moment she looked
at the car, then bolted right at it,
glancing off the hood with a crash,
into a field of corn stubble.

So I rushed at your illness, your
suffering and death—the bright
lights of annihilation and release.

Insomnia at the Solstice

The quicksilver song
of the wood thrush spills
downhill from ancient maples
at the end of the sun's single most
altruistic day. The woods grow dusky
while the bird's song brightens.

Reading to get sleepy . . . Rabbit
Angstrom knows himself so well,
why isn't he a better man?
I turn out the light, and rejoice
in the sound of high summer, and in air
on bare shoulders—*dolce, dolce*—
no blanket, or even a sheet.
A faint glow remains over the lake.

Now come wordless contemplations
on love and death, worry about
money, and the resolve to have the vet
clean the dog's teeth, though
he'll have to anesthetize him.

An easy rain begins, drips off
the edge of the roof, onto the tin
watering can. A vast irritation rises. . . .
I turn and turn, try one pillow,
two, think of people who have no beds.

A car hisses by on wet macadam.
Then another. The room turns
gray by insensible degrees. The thrush

begins again its outpouring of silver
to rich and poor alike, to the just
and the unjust.

The dog's wet nose appears
on the pillow, pressing lightly,
decorously. He needs to go out.
All right, cleverhead, let's declare
a new day.
      Washing up, I say
to the face in the mirror,
"You're still here! How you bored me
all night, and now I'll have
to entertain you all day. . . ."

Peonies at Dusk

White peonies blooming along the porch
send out light
while the rest of the yard grows dim.

Outrageous flowers as big as human
heads! They're staggered
by their own luxuriance: I had
to prop them up with stakes and twine.

The moist air intensifies their scent,
and the moon moves around the barn
to find out what it's coming from.

In the darkening June evening
I draw a blossom near, and bending close
search it as a woman searches
a loved one's face.

The Secret

In a glass case marked "Estate Jewelry"
I see a ring that seems familiar,
remembered, though I've never seen
anything like it.

I ask the clerk, stout and garrulous
behind the counter, to take it out.

The honeybee, with opal body, garnet
head, and golden wings, slides past
my knuckle burled with middle age.

That one antenna is broken
only endears it to me. Still
it climbs into the flower's throat,
and flies, heavy with nectar, back
to its queen. . . .

For weeks I have felt on the point
of learning a mystery, but now
my agitation has dropped away.

IV

Watch Ye, Watch Ye

and be ready to meet me,
for lo, I come at noonday.
Fear ye not, fear ye not
for with my hand I will lead you on,
and safely I'll guide your little boat
beyond this vale of sorrow.

Shaker Hymn

Three Small Oranges

My old flannel nightgown, the elbows out,
one shoulder torn. . . . Instead of putting it
away with the clean wash, I cut it up
for rags, removing the arms and opening
their seams, scissoring across the breast
and upper back, then tearing the thin
cloth of the body into long rectangles.
Suddenly an immense sadness . . .

Making supper, I listen to news
from the war, of torture where the air
is black at noon with burning oil,
and of a market in Baghdad, bombed
by accident, where yesterday an old man
carried in his basket a piece of fish
wrapped in paper and tied with string,
and three small hard green oranges.

A Portion of History

The sweet breath of someone's laundry
spews from a dryer vent. A screen door
slams. "Carry it?"—a woman's voice—
"You're going to *carry* it!?" Now I hear
the sound of casters on the sidewalk.

Car doors close softly, engines
turn over and catch. A boy on his bike
delivers papers, I hear the smack
of the *New York Times* in its blue plastic
sheath, hitting the wooden porches.

In the next street a garbage truck cries out.
A woman jogs by, thrusting a child
in a stroller ahead of her, her arms
straight as shafts, the baby's fair
head bobbing wildly on its frail stem.

Potato

In haste one evening while making dinner
I threw away a potato that was spoiled
on one end. The rest would have been

redeemable. In the yellow garbage pail
it became the consort of coffee grounds,
banana skins, carrot peelings.
I pitched it onto the compost
where steaming scraps and leaves
return, like bodies over time, to earth.

When I flipped the fetid layers with a hay
fork to air the pile, the potato turned up
unfailingly, as if to revile me—

looking plumper, firmer, resurrected
instead of disassembling. It seemed to grow
until I might have made shepherd's pie
for a whole hamlet, people who pass the day
dropping trees, pumping gas, pinning
hand-me-down clothes on the line.

Sleepers in Jaipur

A mango moon climbs the dark
blue sky. In the gutters of a market
a white, untethered cow browses
the day's leavings—wilted greens,
banana peels, spilt rice,
a broken basket.

The sleepers, oh, so many sleepers . . .
They lie on rush mats in their hot
stick hut. The man and woman
want to love wildly, uproariously;
instead, they are quiet and efficient
in the dark. Bangles ring
as his mother stirs in her sleep.

Who can say what will come of
the quickening and slowing
of their breaths on each other's
necks, of their deep shudders?
Another sleeper, a gift of God,
ribs and shoulders to be clothed
in flesh . . .

In the dusty garden the water
she carried from the well in a jug
balanced on her black hair
stares back at the moon
from its cool terra-cotta urn.

Gettysburg: July 1, 1863

The young man, hardly more
than a boy, who fired the shot
had looked at him with an air
not of anger but of concentration,
as if he were surveying a road,
or feeding a length of wood into a saw:
It had to be done just so.

The bullet passed through
his upper chest, below the collarbone.
The pain was not what he might
have feared. Strangely exhilarated
he staggered out of the pasture
and into a grove of trees.

He pressed and pressed
the wound, trying to stanch
the blood, but he could only press
what he could reach, and he could
not reach his back, where the bullet
had exited.
        He lay on the earth
smelling the leaves and mosses,
musty and damp and cool
after the blaze of open afternoon.

How good the earth smelled,
as it had when he was a boy
hiding from his father,
who was intent on strapping him

for doing his chores
late one time too many.

A cowbird razzed from a rail fence.
It isn't mockery, he thought,
no malice in it . . . just a noise.
Stray bullets nicked the oaks
overhead. Leaves and splinters fell.

Someone near him groaned.
But it was his own voice he heard.
His fingers and feet tingled,
the roof of his mouth,
and the bridge of his nose. . . .

He became dry, dry, and thought
of Christ, who said, *I thirst*.
His man-smell, the smell of his hair
and skin, his sweat, the salt smell
of his cock and the little ferny hairs
that two women had known

left him, and a sharp, almost sweet
smell began to rise from his open mouth
in the warm shade of the oaks.
A streak of sun climbed the rough
trunk of a tree, but he did not
see it with his open eye.

Pharaoh

"The future ain't what it used to be,"
said the sage of the New York Yankees
as he pounded his mitt, releasing
the red dust of the infield
into the harshly illuminated evening air.

Big hands. Men with big hands
make things happen. The surgeon,
when I asked how big your tumor was,
held forth his substantial fist
with its globed class ring.

Home again, we live as charily as strangers.
Things are off: Touch rankles, food
is not good. Even the kindness of friends
turns burdensome; their flowers sadden
us, so many and so fair.

I woke in the night to see your
diminished bulk lying beside me—
you on your back, like a sarcophagus
as your feet held up the covers. . . .
The things you might need in the next
life surrounded you—your comb and glasses,
water, a book and a pen.

Otherwise

I got out of bed
on two strong legs.
It might have been
otherwise. I ate
cereal, sweet
milk, ripe, flawless
peach. It might
have been otherwise.
I took the dog uphill
to the birch wood.
All morning I did
the work I love.

At noon I lay down
with my mate. It might
have been otherwise.
We ate dinner together
at a table with silver
candlesticks. It might
have been otherwise.
I slept in a bed
in a room with paintings
on the walls, and
planned another day
just like this day.
But one day, I know,
it will be otherwise.

Notes from the Other Side

I divested myself of despair
and fear when I came here.

Now there is no more catching
one's own eye in the mirror,

there are no bad books, no plastic,
no insurance premiums, and of course

no illness. Contrition
does not exist, nor gnashing

of teeth. No one howls as the first
clod of earth hits the casket.

The poor we no longer have with us.
Our calm hearts strike only the hour,

and God, as promised, proves
to be mercy clothed in light.

Last Poems

in

Otherwise
(1996)

and in

A Hundred White Daffodils
(1999)

Happiness

There's just no accounting for happiness,
or the way it turns up like a prodigal
who comes back to the dust at your feet
having squandered a fortune far away.

And how can you not forgive?
You make a feast in honor of what
was lost, and take from its place the finest
garment, which you saved for an occasion
you could not imagine, and you weep night and day
to know that you were not abandoned,
that happiness saved its most extreme form
for you alone.

No, happiness is the uncle you never
knew about, who flies a single-engine plane
onto the grassy landing strip, hitchhikes
into town, and inquires at every door
until he finds you asleep midafternoon
as you so often are during the unmerciful
hours of your despair.

It comes to the monk in his cell.
It comes to the woman sweeping the street
with a birch broom, to the child
whose mother has passed out from drink.
It comes to the lover, to the dog chewing
a sock, to the pusher, to the basket maker,

and to the clerk stacking cans of carrots
in the night.
           It even comes to the boulder
in the perpetual shade of pine barrens,
to rain falling on the open sea,
to the wineglass, weary of holding wine.

Mosaic of the Nativity: Serbia, Winter 1993

On the domed ceiling God
is thinking:
I made them my joy,
and everything else I created
I made to bless them.
But see what they do!
I know their hearts
and arguments:

"We're descended from
Cain. Evil is nothing new,
so what does it matter now
if we shell the infirmary,
and the well where the fearful
and rash alike must
come for water?"

God thinks Mary into being.
Suspended at the apogee
of the golden dome,
she curls in a brown pod,
and inside her the mind
of Christ, cloaked in blood,
lodges and begins to grow.

Man Eating

The man at the table across from mine
is eating yogurt. His eyes, following
the progress of the spoon, cross briefly
each time it nears his face. Time,

and the world with all its principalities,
might come to an end as prophesied
by the Apostle John, but what about
this man, so completely present

to the little carton with its cool,
sweet food, which has caused no animal
to suffer, and which he is eating
with a pearl-white plastic spoon.

Man Waking

The room was already light when
he awoke, and his body curled
like a grub suddenly exposed
when something dislodges a stone.
Work. He was more than an hour
late. Let that pass, he thought.
He pulled the covers over his head.
The smell of his skin and hair
offended him. Now he drew his legs
up a little more, and sent
his forehead down to meet his knees.
His knees felt cool.
A surprising amount of light
came through the blanket. He could
easily see his hand. Not dark enough,
not the utter darkness he desired.

Man Sleeping

Large flakes of snow fall slowly, far
apart, like whales who cannot find mates
in the vast blue latitudes.

Why do I think of the man asleep
on the grassy bank outside the Sackler
Museum in Washington?
                                        It was a chill
afternoon. He lay, no doubt, on everything
he owned, belly-down, his head twisted
awkwardly to the right, mouth open
in abandon.
                        He looked
like a child who has fallen asleep
still dressed on the top of the covers,
or like Abel, broken, at his brother's feet.

Cesarean

The surgeon with his unapologetic
blade parted darkness, revealing
day. Then from her large clay
he drew toward his masked
face my small clay. The clatter,
the white light, the vast freedom
were terrible. Outside in, oh, inside
out, and why did everybody shout?

Surprise

He suggests pancakes at the local diner,
followed by a walk in search of mayflowers,
while friends convene at the house
bearing casseroles and a cake, their cars
pulled close along the sandy shoulders
of the road, where tender ferns unfurl
in the ditches, and this year's budding leaves
push last year's spectral leaves from the tips
of the twigs of the ash trees. The gathering
itself is not what astounds her, but the casual
accomplishment with which he has lied.

No

The last prayer had been said,
and it was time to turn away
from the casket, poised on its silver
scaffolding over the open hole
that smelled like a harrowed field.

And then I heard a noise that seemed
not to be human. It was more like wind
among leafless trees, or cattle lowing
in a distant barn. I paused with one
hand on the roof of the car,

while the sound rose in pitch, then
cohered into language: *No, don't do this
to me! No, no . . . !* And each of us
stood where we were, unsure
whether to stay, or leave her there.

Drawing from the Past

Only Mama and I were at home.
We ate tomato sandwiches
with sweeps of mayonnaise
on indifferent white bread.

Surely it was September,
my older brother at school.
The tomatoes were fragrant
and richly red, perhaps the last
before frost.

I was alert to the joy of eating
sandwiches alone with Mama, bare
feet braced on the underpinnings
of the abraded kitchen table.

Once I'd made a mark in the wood
by pressing too hard as I traced
the outline of a horse.

I was no good at drawing—from life,
or from imagination. My brother
was good at it, and I was alert
to that, too.

The Call

I lunged out of sleep toward the ringing
phone, from a dream in which, carrying
plastic bags of her inhalers,
I struggled up the icy drive.

Still startled, I sit up in bed
in the dark with my glasses on.
The clock's blue spectral glow says 4:13.
He's speeding now to the nursing home
with the clarity that fear alone
confers, to see his mother, it may be,
for the last time. Rain has fallen

all night, and the intimate
smells of wet earth press through
the screen. A sudden stir of air moves
the sere late summer leaves, sounding
for a moment like still more rain.

In the Nursing Home

She is like a horse grazing
a hill pasture that someone makes
smaller by coming every night
to pull the fences in and in.

She has stopped running wide loops,
stopped even the tight circles.
She drops her head to feed; grass
is dust, and the creekbed's dry.

Master, come with your light
halter. Come and bring her in.

How Like the Sound

How like the sound of laughing weeping
is. I wasn't sure until I saw your face—
your eyes squeezed shut, and the big
hot tears spurting out.

There you sat, upright, in your mother's
reclining chair, tattered from the wear
of many years. Not since childhood
had you wept this way, head back, throat

open like a hound. Of course the howling
had to stop. I saw you add *call realtor*
to your list before your red face
vanished behind the morning *Register.*

Eating the Cookies

The cousin from Maine, knowing
about her diverticulitis, left out the nuts,
so the cookies weren't entirely to my taste,
but they were good enough; yes, good enough.

Each time I emptied a drawer or shelf
I permitted myself to eat one.
I cleared the closet of silk caftans
that slipped easily from clattering hangers,
and from the bureau I took her nightgowns
and sweaters, financial documents
neatly cinctured in long gray envelopes,
and the hairnets and peppermints she'd tucked among
Lucite frames abounding with great-grandchildren,
solemn in their Christmas finery.

Finally the drawers were empty,
the bags full, and the largest cookie,
which I had saved for last, lay
solitary in the tin with a nimbus
of crumbs around it. There would be no more
parcels from Portland. I took it up
and sniffed it, and before eating it,
pressed it against my forehead, because
it seemed like the next thing to do.

Spring Evening

Again the thrush affirms
both dusk and dawn. The frog
releases spawn in the warm
inlet of the pond. Ferns
rise with the crescent moon,
and the old farmer
waits to sow his corn.

Prognosis

I walked alone in the chill of dawn
while my mind leapt, as the teachers

of detachment say, like a drunken
monkey. Then a gray shape, an owl,

passed overhead. An owl is not
like a crow. A crow makes convivial

chuckings as it flies,
but the owl flew well beyond me

before I heard it coming, and when it
settled, the bough did not sway.

Afternoon at MacDowell

On a windy summer day the well-dressed
trustees occupy the first row
under the yellow and white striped canopy.
Their drive for capital is over,
and for a while this refuge is secure.

Thin after your second surgery, you wear
the gray summer suit we bought eight
years ago for momentous occasions
in warm weather. My hands rest in my lap,
under the fine cotton shawl embroidered
with mirrors that we bargained for last fall
in Bombay, unaware of your sickness.

The legs of our chairs poke holes
in the lawn. The sun goes in and out
of the grand clouds, making the air alive
with golden light, and then, as if heaven's
spirits had fallen, everything's somber again.

After music and poetry we walk to the car.
I believe in the miracles of art, but what
prodigy will keep you safe beside me,
fumbling with the radio while you drive
to find late innings of a Red Sox game?

Fat

The doctor says it's better for my spine
this way—more fat, more estrogen.
Well, then! There was a time when a wife's
plump shoulders signified prosperity.

These days my fashionable friends
get by on seaweed milkshakes,
Pall Malls, and vitamin pills. Their clothes
hang elegantly from their clavicles.

As the evening news makes clear
the starving and the besieged maintain
the current standard of beauty without effort.

Whenever two or three gather together
the talk turns dreamily to sausages,
purple cabbages, black beans and rice,
noodles gleaming with cream, yams, and plums,
and chapati fried in ghee.

The Way Things Are in Franklin

Even the undertaker is going out
of business. And since the dime store closed,
we can't get parakeets on Main Street
anymore, or sleeveless gingham smocks
for keeping Church Fair pie off the ample
fronts of the strong, garrulous wives
of pipefitters and road agents.
The hardware's done for too.
                                    Yesterday,
a Sunday, I saw the proprietors breaking
up shop, the woman struggling with half
a dozen bicycle tires on each arm,
like bangle bracelets, the man balancing
boxes filled with Teflon pans. The windows
had been soaped to frustrate curiosity,
or pity, or that cheerless satisfaction
we sometimes feel when others fail.

Dutch Interiors

for Caroline

Christ has been done to death
in the cold reaches of northern Europe
a thousand thousand times.
                              Suddenly bread
and cheese appear on a plate
beside a gleaming pewter beaker of beer.

Now tell me that the Holy Ghost
does not reside in the play of light
on cutlery!

A woman makes lace,
with a moist-eyed spaniel lying
at her small shapely feet.
Even the maid with the chamber pot
is here; the naughty, red-cheeked girl. . . .

And the merchant's wife, still
in her yellow dressing gown
at noon, dips her quill into India ink
with an air of cautious pleasure.

Reading Aloud to My Father

I chose the book haphazard
from the shelf, but with Nabokov's first
sentence I knew it wasn't the thing
to read to a dying man:
The cradle rocks above an abyss, it began,
and common sense tells us that our existence
is but a brief crack of light
between two eternities of darkness.

The words disturbed both of us immediately,
and I stopped. With music it was the same—
Chopin's Piano Concerto—he asked me
to turn it off. He ceased eating, and drank
little, while the tumors briskly appropriated
what was left of him.

But to return to the cradle rocking. I think
Nabokov had it wrong. This is the abyss.
That's why babies howl at birth,
and why the dying so often reach
for something only they can apprehend.

At the end they don't want their hands
to be under the covers, and if you should put
your hand on theirs in a tentative gesture
of solidarity, they'll pull the hand free;
and you must honor that desire,
and let them pull it free.

Woman, Why Are You Weeping?

The morning after the crucifixion,
Mary Magdalene came to see the body
of Christ. She found the stone
rolled away from an empty tomb. Two
figures dressed in white asked her,
"Woman, why are you weeping?"

"Because," she replied, "they have
taken away my Lord, and I don't know
where they have laid him."

Returned from long travel, I sit
in the familiar, sun-streaked pew, waiting
for the bread and wine of Holy Communion.
The old comfort does not rise in me, only
apathy and bafflement.
                              India, with her ceaseless
bells and fire; her crows calling stridently
all night; India with her sandalwood
smoke, and graceful gods, many-headed and many-
armed, has taken away the one who blessed
and kept me.
                    The thing is done, as surely
as if my luggage had been stolen from the train.
Men and women with faces as calm as lakes at dusk
have taken away my Lord, and I don't know
where to find him.

❥

What is Brahman? I don't know Brahman.
I don't know *saccidandana,* the bliss
of the absolute and unknowable.
I only know that I have lost the Lord
in whose image I was made.

Whom shall I thank for this pear,
sweet and white? Food *is* God, *Prasadam,*
God's mercy. But who is this God?
The one who is *not this, not that?*

The absurdity of all religious forms
breaks over me, as the absurdity of language
made me feel faint the day I heard friends
giving commands to their neighbor's dog
in Spanish. . . . At first I laughed,
but then I became frightened.

❧

They have taken away my Lord, a person
whose life I held inside me. I saw him
heal, and teach, and eat among sinners.
I saw him break the sabbath to make a higher
sabbath. I saw him lose his temper.

I knew his anguish when he called, "I thirst!"
and received vinegar to drink. The Bible
does not say it, but I am sure he turned
his head away. Not long after he cried, "My God,
my God, why have you forsaken me?"

I watched him reveal himself risen
to Magdalene with a single word: "Mary!"

It was my habit to speak to him. His goodness
perfumed my life. I loved the Lord, he heard
my cry, and he loved me as his own.

～

A man sleeps on the pavement, on a raffia mat—
the only thing that has not been stolen from him.
This stranger who loves what cannot be understood
has put out my light with his calm face.

Shall the fire answer my fears and vapors?
The fire cares nothing for my illness,
nor does Brahma, the creator, nor Shiva who sees
evil with his terrible third eye; Vishnu,
the protector, does not protect me.

I've brought home the smell of the streets
in the folds of soft, bright cotton garments.
When I iron them the steam brings back
the complex odors that rise from the gutters,
of tuberoses, urine, dust, joss, and death.

～

On a curb in Allahabad the family gathers
under a dusty tree, a few quilts hung
between lightposts and a wattle fence
for privacy. Eleven sit or lie around the fire

while a woman of sixty stirs a huge pot.
Rice cooks in a narrow-necked crock
on the embers. A small dog, with patches of bald,
red skin on his back, lies on the corner
of the piece of canvas that serves as flooring.

Looking at them I lose my place.
I don't know why I was born, or why
I live in a house in New England, or why I am
a visitor with heavy luggage giving lectures
for the State Department. Why am I not
tap-tapping with my fingernail
on the rolled-up window of a white Government car,
a baby in my arms, drugged to look feverish?

Rajiv did not weep. He did not cover
his face with his hands when we rowed past
the dead body of a newborn nudging the grassy
banks at Benares—close by a snake
rearing up, and a cast-off garland of flowers.

He explained. When a family are too poor
to cremate their dead, they bring the body
here, and slip it into the waters of the Ganges
and Yamuna rivers.
                    Perhaps the child was dead
at birth; perhaps it had the misfortune
to be born a girl. The mother may have walked
two days with her baby's body to this place
where Gandhi's ashes once struck the waves

with a sound like gravel being scuffed
over the edge of a bridge.

"What shall we do about this?" I asked
my God, who even then was leaving me. The reply
was scorching wind, lapping of water, pull
of the black oarsmen on the oars. . . .

The Sick Wife

The sick wife stayed in the car
while he bought a few groceries.
Not yet fifty,
she had learned what it's like
not to be able to button a button.

It was the middle of the day—
and so only mothers with small children
or retired couples
stepped through the muddy parking lot.

Dry cleaning swung and gleamed on hangers
in the cars of the prosperous.
How easily they moved—
with such freedom,
even the old and relatively infirm.

The windows began to steam up.
The cars on either side of her
pulled away so briskly
that it made her sick at heart.

Uncollected Poems

What It's Like

And once, for no special reason,
I rode in the back of the pickup,
leaning against the cab.
Everything familiar was receding
fast—the mountain,
the motel, Huldah Currier's
house, and the two stately maples. . . .

Mr. Perkins was having a barn sale,
and cars from New Jersey and Ohio
were parked along the sandy shoulder
of Route 4. Whatever I saw
I had already passed. . . .
(This must be what life is like
at the moment of leaving it.)

Indolence in Early Winter

A letter arrives from friends. . . .
Let them all divorce, remarry
and divorce again!
Forgive me if I doze off in my chair.

I should have stoked the stove
an hour ago. The house
will go cold as stone. Wonderful!
I won't have to go on
balancing my checkbook.

Unanswered mail piles up
in drifts, precarious,
and the cat sets everything sliding
when she comes to see me.

I am still here in my chair,
buried under the rubble
of failed marriages, magazine
subscription renewal forms, bills,
lapsed friendships. . . .

This kind of thinking is caused
by the sun. It leaves the sky earlier
every day, and goes off somewhere,
like a troubled husband,
or like a melancholy wife.

Breakfast at the Mount Washington Hotel

In the valley a warm spring rain. . . .
Mount Washington, blue, but with snow
still gleaming in the ravines,
looks equably down on the old hotel,
which is painted white, and on dreary days
seems to emit light. Its long porch,
weathered like the deck of a ship, proffers
empty wicker rocking chairs
madly ajog in the mizzly breeze.

At the turn of the century
those who arrived by motorcar
came to a separate entrance,
so the horses on the bridlepaths
would not be frightened. All very grand . . .
and by now slightly shabby
in a European way.

Only the young—just married, and looking
shyly down—or the prosperous stay here.
We are the anomaly.
The waiter comes with coffee . . . the cups
are large, and thin at the edge. In the easy
silence of our twelfth anniversary
we look out at the mountain. Swallows dip
and tilt under the portico. After all
it's time for them
to choose a mate and build a nest. . . .

A tense man in a three-piece suit
sets out round metal tables in the rain.
Everything is in place. After Memorial Day
the real summer season will begin.

At the IGA: Franklin, New Hampshire

This is where I would shop
if my husband worked felling trees
for the mill, hurting himself badly
from time to time; where I would bring
my three kids; where I would push
one basket and pull another
because the boxes of diapers and cereal
and gallon milk jugs take so much room.

I would already have put the clothes
in the two largest washers next door
at the Norge Laundry Village. Done shopping,
I'd pile the wet wash in trash bags
and take it home to dry on the line.

And I would think, hanging out the baby's
shirts and sleepers, and cranking the pulley
away from me, how it would be
to change lives with someone,
like the woman who came after us
in the checkout, thin, with lots of rings
on her hands, who looked us over openly.

Things would have been different
if I hadn't let Bob climb on top of me
for ninety seconds in 1979.
It was raining lightly in the state park
and so we were alone. The charcoal fire
hissed as the first drops fell. . . .
In ninety seconds we made this life—

a trailer on a windy hill, dangerous jobs
in the woods or night work at the packing plant;
Roy, Kimberly, Bobby; too much in the hamper,
never enough in the bank.

Translations

Twenty Poems of Anna Akhmatova

(1985)

Translated from the Russian
by Jane Kenyon
with Vera Sandomirsky Dunham

— for my mother
and in memory of my father

Introduction (1984)

As we remember Keats for the beauty and intensity of his shorter poems, especially the odes and sonnets, so we revere Akhmatova for her early lyrics—brief, perfectly made verses of passion and feeling. Images build emotional pressure:

> And sweeter even than the singing of songs
> is this dream, now becoming real:
> the swaying of branches brushed aside
> and the faint ringing of your spurs.

I love the sudden twists these poems take, often in the last line. In one poem the recollection of a literary party ends with the first frank exchange of glances between lovers. Another poem lists sweet-smelling things—mignonette, violets, apples—and ends, astonishingly, ". . . we have found out forever/that blood smells only of blood." These poems celebrate the sensual life, and Akhmatova's devoted attention to details of sense always serves feeling:

> With the hissing of a snake the scythe cuts down
> the stalks, one pressed hard against another.

The snake's hissing is accurate to the sound of scythe mowing, and more than accurate: by using the snake for her auditory image, Akhmatova compares this rural place, where love has gone awry, to the lost Eden.

Akhmatova was born Anna Gorenko near Odessa in 1889. Soon her family moved to Tsarskoe Selo, near St. Petersburg, and there she began her education. Studying French, she learned to love Baudelaire and Verlaine. At the age of ten she became seriously ill, with a disease never diagnosed, and went deaf for a brief time. As she recovered she wrote her first poems.

Money was not abundant in the Gorenko household, nor was tranquility. Akhmatova did not get on with her father, Andrei Gorenko, a naval engineer who lectured at the Naval Academy in St. Petersburg—also a notorious philanderer whose money went to his mistresses. (We know little of Akhmatova's relationship with her mother.) Akhmatova's brother Victor recalls an occasion when the young girl asked their father for money for a new coat. When he refused she threw off her clothes and became hysterical. (See *Akhmatova: Poems, Correspondence, Reminiscences, Iconography:* Ardis.) Andrei Gorenko deserted his family in 1905. A few years later, hearing that his daughter wrote verse, he asked her to choose a pen name. He wished to avoid the ignominy, as he put it, of "a decadent poetess" in the family. She took her Tartar great-grandmother's name.

When Akhmatova was still a schoolgirl she met Nikolai Gumilev, a poet and founder of Acmeism who became her mentor and her first husband. Nadezhda Mandelstam has said that Akhmatova rarely spoke of her childhood; she seemed to consider her marriage to Gumilev the beginning of her life. (See Mandelstam's *Hope Abandoned:* Atheneum.) She was slow to accept his proposal. He sought her attention by repeated attempts at suicide until she finally married him in 1910. The bride's family did not attend the ceremony. Having won her at last, Gumilev promptly left to spend six months in Africa. On his return, while still at the train station, he asked her if she had been writing. By reply she handed him the manuscript of *Evening,* her first book.

Their son, Lev Gumilev, was born in 1912, the same year Akhmatova published *Evening.* By 1917, when she was twenty-eight, she had brought out two more books, *Rosary* and *White Flock.* Despite the historical tumult of World War I and the Revolution, her poetry quickly became popular. But tumult was private as well as public: by 1918 her marriage had failed; Akhmatova divorced Gumilev and the same autumn married the Assyriologist V. K. Shileiko. This unhappy alliance—Shileiko burned his wife's poems in the samovar—lasted for six years. (See Amanda Haight's biography, *Akhmatova: A Poetic Pilgrimage:* Oxford.) Ordinary family life eluded Akhmatova, who went through many love affairs. Before her divorce from Shileiko, she lived in a ménage à trois with Nikolai Punin and his wife; Punin later became her third husband. Motherhood was not easy. ("The lot of a mother is a bright torture: I was not worthy of it. . . .") For the most part, Gumilev's mother raised her grandson Lev.

In the years following her early triumphs Akhmatova suffered many torments, as the Soviet regime hardened into tyranny. Gumilev was executed in 1921 for alleged anti-Bolshevik activity. Early in the twenties Soviet critics denounced Akhmatova's work as anachronistic and useless to the Revolution. The Central Committee of the Communist Party forbade publication of her verse; from 1923 to 1940, none of her poetry appeared in print. The great poems of her maturity, *Requiem,* and *Song Without a Hero,* exist in Russia today only by underground publication, or *samizdat.*

During the Stalinist terror of the 1930s the poet's son Lev and her husband Punin were imprisoned. Akhmatova's fellow Acmeist and close friend Osip Mandelstam died in a prison camp in 1938. (Punin died in another camp fifteen years later.) During the Second World War the Committee of the Communist Party of Leningrad evacuated Akhmatova to Tashkent in Uzbekistan. There she lived in a small, hot room, in ill health, with Osip Mandelstam's widow Nadezhda.

In 1944 Akhmatova returned to Leningrad, to a still-higher wave of official antagonism. In a prominent literary magazine, Andrei Zhdanov denounced her as ". . . a frantic little fine lady flitting between the boudoir and the chapel . . . half-nun, half-harlot." The Union of Soviet Writers expelled her. A new book of poems, already in print, was seized and destroyed. For many years she supported herself only by working as a translator from Asiatic languages and from French, an activity she compared to "eating one's own brain" (Haight).

The final decade of her life was relatively tranquil. During the thaw that followed Stalin's death, the government released Lev Gumilev from labor camp and reinstated Akhmatova in the Writer's Union. She was permitted to publish and to travel. In Italy and England she received honors and saw old friends. She died in March 1966, and was buried at Komarovo, near Leningrad.

Akhmatova's work ranges from the highly personal early lyrics through the longer, more public and political *Requiem,* on to the allusive and cryptic *Poem Without a Hero.* The early poems embody Acmeist principles. Acmeism grew out of the Poet's Guild, which Nikolai Gumilev and Sergei Gorodetsky founded in 1912—fifteen poets who met regularly to read poems and argue aesthetic theory. At one meeting, Gumilev proposed an attack on Symbolism with its "obligatory mysticism." He proposed Acmeism as an alternative; Acmeism held that a rose is beautiful in itself, not because it stands for something. These poets announced that they were craftsmen not priests, and dedicated themselves to clarity, concision, and perfection of form. They summed up their goals in two words: "beautiful clarity." Gumilev himself, Akhmatova, and Osip Mandelstam were the leading Acmeists, and the movement thrived for a decade.

Written so many years later, *Requiem* and *Poem Without a Hero* naturally moved past Akhmatova's early poems in intention and in scope. They are manifestly political and historical. *Requiem* records the terror of the purges in the 1930s, commemorating the women who stood waiting outside prison gates with parcels for husbands, sons, and brothers; Akhmatova compares the suffering of these women to Mary's at the Crucifixion. In the prefatory note to *Poem Without a Hero* Akhmatova says: "I dedicate this poem to its first listeners—my friends and countrymen who perished in Leningrad during the siege."

These translations are free-verse versions of rhymed and metered poems. Losing the formal perfection of the Russian verses—much of the "beautiful clarity"—has been a constant source of frustration and sadness to me and to my co-worker, Vera Sandomirsky Dunham. But something, I think, crosses the barrier between our languages.

Because it is impossible to translate with fidelity to form *and* to image, I have sacrificed form for image. Image embodies feeling, and this embodiment is perhaps the greatest treasure of lyric poetry. In translating, I mean to place the integrity of the image over all other considerations.

Translation provides many frustrations. It seems impossible to translate a single Russian syllable that means "What did he have to do that for?" Trying to translate lines about a native place—so important to Akhmatova, who firmly refused expatriation—how does one render *rodnoi,* which means "all that is dear to me, familiar, my own . . ."? I remember Vera clapping her hands to her head and moaning, "This will sink us. . . ."

There are times when—in the interest of cadence, tone, or clarity—I have altered punctuation or moved something from one line to another. Often I needed to shift the verb from the end to the beginning of the sentence. Sometimes a word, translated from Russian as the dictionary would have it, made impossible English. I list significant variations from the original in notes at the back of this book. We have translated from the two volume *Works,* edited by G. P. Struve and B. A. Filippov, published by Interlanguage Literary Associates in 1965.

I want to thank Robert Bly, who first encouraged me to read Akhmatova, and later to translate these poems. I also thank Lou Teel, who, as a student of Russian at Dartmouth, helped me begin the work. I owe special thanks to Vera Sandomirsky Dunham, a busy scholar, teacher, and lifelong lover of these poems. Her fear that a free-verse translation of Akhmatova is fundamentally misconceived has not prevented her from offering her time, her erudition, and her hospitality.

J. K.

Poems from

Evening (1912)

Rosary (1914)

White Flock (1917)

≈

I

The memory of sun weakens in my heart,
grass turns yellow,
wind blows the early flakes of snow
lightly, lightly.

Already the narrow canals have stopped flowing;
water freezes.
Nothing will ever happen here—
not ever!

Against the empty sky the willow opens
a transparent fan.
Maybe it's a good thing I'm not
your wife.

The memory of sun weakens in my heart.
What's this? Darkness?
It's possible. And this may be the first night
of winter.

1911

2

Evening hours at the desk.
And a page irreparably white.
The mimosa calls up the heat of Nice,
a large bird flies in a beam of moonlight.

And having braided my hair carefully for the night
as if tomorrow braids will be necessary,
I look out the window, no longer sad,—
at the sea, the sandy slopes.

What power a man has
who doesn't ask for tenderness!
I cannot lift my tired eyes
when he speaks my name.

1913

3

I know, I know the skis
will begin again their dry creaking.
In the dark blue sky the moon is red,
and the meadow slopes so sweetly.

The windows of the palace burn
remote and still.
No path, no lane,
only the iceholes are dark.

Willow, tree of nymphs,
don't get in my way.
Shelter the black grackles, black
grackles among your snowy branches.

1913

4

The Guest

Everything's just as it was: fine hard snow
beats against the dining room windows,
and I myself have not changed:
even so, a man came to call.

I asked him: "What do you want?"
He said, "To be with you in hell."
I laughed: "It seems you see
plenty of trouble ahead for us both."

But lifting his dry hand
he lightly touched the flowers.
"Tell me how they kiss you,
tell me how you kiss."

And his half-closed eyes
remained on my ring.
Not even the smallest muscle moved
in his serenely angry face.

Oh, I know it fills him with joy—
this hard and passionate certainty
that there is nothing he needs,
and nothing I can keep from him.

1 January 1914

5

N.V.N.

There is a sacred, secret line in loving
which attraction and even passion cannot cross,—
even if lips draw near in awful silence
and love tears at the heart.

Friendship is weak and useless here,
and years of happiness, exalted and full of fire,
because the soul is free and does not know
the slow luxuries of sensual life.

Those who try to come near it are insane
and those who reach it are shaken by grief.
So now you know exactly why
my heart beats no faster under your hand.

1915

6

Like a white stone in a deep well
one memory lies inside me.
I cannot and will not fight against it:
it is joy and it is pain.

It seems to me that anyone who looks
into my eyes will notice it immediately,
becoming sadder and more pensive
than someone listening to a melancholy tale.

I remember how the gods turned people
into things, not killing their consciousness.
And now, to keep these glorious sorrows alive,
you have turned into my memory of you.

1916
Slepnevo

7

Everything promised him to me:
the fading amber edge of the sky,
and the sweet dreams of Christmas,
and the wind at Easter, loud with bells,

and the red shoots of the grapevine,
and waterfalls in the park,
and two large dragonflies
on the rusty iron fencepost.

And I could only believe
that he would be mine
as I walked along the high slopes,
the path of burning stones.

1916

Poems from

Plantain (1921)

8

Yes I loved them, those gatherings late at night,—
the small table, glasses with frosted sides,
fragrant vapor rising from black coffee,
the fireplace, red with powerful winter heat,
the biting gaiety of a literary joke,
and the first helpless and frightening glance of my love.

1917

9

Twenty-first. Night. Monday.
Silhouette of the capitol in darkness.
Some good-for-nothing—who knows why—
made up the tale that love exists on earth.

People believe it, maybe from laziness
or boredom, and live accordingly:
they wait eagerly for meetings, fear parting,
and when they sing, they sing about love.

But the secret reveals itself to some,
and on them silence settles down. . . .
I found this out by accident
and now it seems I'm sick all the time.

1917

10

There is a certain hour every day
so troubled and heavy . . .
I speak to melancholy in a loud voice
not bothering to open my sleepy eyes.
And it pulses like blood,
is warm like a sigh,
like happy love
is smart and nasty.

1917

II

We walk along the hard crest of the snowdrift
toward my white, mysterious house,
both of us so quiet,
keeping the silence as we go along.
And sweeter even than the singing of songs
is this dream, now becoming real:
the swaying of branches brushed aside
and the faint ringing of your spurs.

January 1917

12

All day the crowd rushes one way, then another;
its own gasping frightens it still more,
and laughing skulls fly on funereal banners,
prophesying from the river's far side.
For this I sang and dreamed!
They have torn my heart in two.
How quiet it is after the volley!
Death sends patrols into every courtyard.

1917

13

The river flows without hurry through the valley,
a house with many windows rises on the hill—
and we live as people did under Catherine;
hold church services at home, wait for harvest.
Two days have passed, two days' separation;
a guest comes riding along a golden wheatfield.
In the parlor he kisses my grandmother's hand,
and on the steep staircase he kisses my lips.

Summer 1917

14

The mysterious spring still lay under a spell,
the transparent wind stalked over the mountains,
and the deep lake kept on being blue,—
a temple of the Baptist not made by hands.

You were frightened by our first meeting,
but I already prayed for the second, and now
the evening is hot, the way it was then. . . .
How close the sun has come to the mountain.

You are not with me, but this is no separation:
to me each instant is—triumphant news.
I know there is such anguish in you
that you cannot say a single word.

Spring 1917

15

I hear the always-sad voice of the oriole
and I salute the passing of delectable summer.
With the hissing of a snake the scythe cuts down
the stalks, one pressed hard against another.

And the hitched-up skirts of the slender reapers
fly in the wind like holiday flags. Now if only
we had the cheerful ring of harness bells,
a lingering glance through dusty eyelashes.

I don't expect caresses or flattering love-talk,
I sense unavoidable darkness coming near,
but come and see the Paradise where together,
blissful and innocent, we once lived.

1917

16

You are an apostate: for a green island
you give away your native land,
our songs and our icons
and the pine tree over the quiet lake.

Why is it, you dashing man from Yaroslav,
if you still have your wits
why are you gaping at the beautiful red-heads
and the luxurious houses?

You might as well be sacrilegious and swagger,
finish off your orthodox soul,
stay where you are in the royal capital
and begin to love your freedom in earnest.

How does it happen that you come to moan
under my small high window?
You know yourself that waves won't drown you
and mortal combat leaves you without a scratch.

It's true that neither the sea nor battles
frighten those who have renounced Paradise.
That's why at the hour of prayer
you asked to be remembered.

1917
Slepnevo

Various Later Poems

17

Wild honey has the scent of freedom,
dust—of a ray of sun,
a girl's mouth—of a violet,
and gold—has no perfume.

Watery—the mignonette,
and like an apple—love,
but we have found out forever
that blood smells only of blood.

.

18

It is not with the lyre of someone in love
that I go seducing people.
The rattle of the leper
is what sings in my hands.

19

Tale of the Black Ring

1

Presents were rare things
coming from my grandmother, a Tartar;
and she was bitterly angry
when I was baptized.
But she turned kind before she died
and for the first time pitied me,
sighing: "Oh the years!
and here my young granddaughter!"
Forgiving my peculiar ways
she left her black ring to me.
She said: "It becomes her,
with this things will be better for her."

2

I said to my friends:
"There is plenty of grief, so little joy."
And I left, covering my face;
I lost the ring.
My friends said:
"We looked everywhere for the ring,
on the sandy shore,
and among pines near the small clearing."
One more daring than the rest
caught up with me on the tree-lined drive
and tried to convince me
to wait for the close of day.
The advice astonished me

and I grew angry with my friend
because his eyes were full of sympathy:
"And what do I need you for?
You can only laugh,
boast in front of the others
and bring flowers."
I told them all to go away.

3

Coming into my cheerful room
I called out like a bird of prey,
fell back on the bed
to remember for the hundredth time
how I sat at supper
and looked into dark eyes,
ate nothing, drank nothing
at the oak table,
how under the regular pattern of the tablecloth
I held out the black ring,
how he looked into my face,
stood up and stepped out onto the porch.

. . . .

They won't come to me with what they have found!
Far over the swiftly moving boat
the sails turned white,
the sky flushed pink.

1917–1936

20

On the Road

Though this land is not my own
I will never forget it,
or the waters of its ocean,
fresh and delicately icy.

Sand on the bottom is whiter than chalk,
and the air drunk, like wine.
Late sun lays bare
the rosy limbs of the pine trees.

And the sun goes down in waves of ether
in such a way that I can't tell
if the day is ending, or the world,
or if the secret of secrets is within me again.

1964

Notes

"The memory of sun weakens in my heart" . . . from *Evening*.
Line 15: Literally, "Maybe! This night will manage to come/winter."

"Evening hours at the desk" . . . from *Rosary*.
Line 3: Literally, "The mimosa smells of Nice and warmth."

"I know, I know the skis" . . . from *Rosary*.
Line 6: Literally, "removed by silence."
Line 8: Holes in the ice made by fishermen . . .

"The Guest" . . . from *Rosary*.
Line 13: Literally, "And his eyes gazing dimly . . ."
Lines 17 and 18: Literally, "Oh I know his bliss is to know (with stress, by force) and passionately . . ."

"There is a sacred, secret line" . . . from *White Flock*.
Line 1: Literally, ". . . in inloveness" . . . "being in love."
Line 3: Literally, ". . . even if lips blend . . ."
Line 5: Literally, ". . . friendship is impotent . . ."
Line 8: Literally, ". . . the slow languor of carnal passion."

"Like a white stone in a deep well" . . . from *White Flock*.

"Everything promised him to me . . ." from *White Flock*.
Line 10: Literally, ". . . that he would be friends with me."
Line 12: Literally, ". . . along the hot, stony path."

"Twenty-first. Night. Monday . . ." from *Plantain*.
Line 3: ". . . who knows why"—literally, ". . . what did he have to do that for?"
Line 8: Literally, ". . . they sing love songs."

"There is a certain hour every day" . . . from *Plantain*.
Line 3: Here translated as melancholy; in the Russian, *toska:* melancholy, yearning, boredom, sweet sadness, all at once. What is more, *toska* has a feminine gender. So *she* pulses like blood, *she's* warm like a sigh, etc., thereby making "sisters" of the speaker and the melancholy to which she addresses herself.

"We walk along the hard crest . . ." from *Plantain*.
In Russian the verb "walk" is delayed until line 4, and is coupled with an adjective meaning "soft" or "tender."
Line 8: Literally, ". . . the tinkling of your spurs."

"All day the crowd rushes . . ." from *Plantain*.
Lines 1 and 2: Literally, "And the whole day, turning frightened of its own gasps, in deadly agitation the crowd rushes."

"The mysterious spring . . ." from *Plantain*.
Line 8: Literally, ". . . how low the sun stands over the mountain."

"You are an apostate . . ." from *Plantain*.
Line 17: Literally, "Yes, neither the sea nor battles . . ."

"Wild honey has the scent of freedom . . ." from Struve, Vol. 2, p. 137. *Poems of Various Years*.
Line 4: Literally, ". . . and gold—of nothing."
Lines 5 and 6: Literally, "Of water smells the mignonette,/and of apple—love." It seemed important to keep the abstractions—freedom and love—in parallel positions within their stanzas. I couldn't bring myself to say "Of water smells the mignonette . . ."—that's not English. So I left out the verb and invented "watery."

"It is not with the lyre of someone in love . . ." from Struve, Vol. 2, p. 139.

"Tale of the Black Ring . . ." from Struve, Vol. 1, p. 180.
For Akhmatova the gift of the ring was synonymous with the gift of song.

Line 3: Grandmother was Muslim and baptism was foreign to her belief.

Line 27: Literally, ". . . his eyes are tender."

"On the Road" from *Odd Number: Verses 1907–1964* (Struve, Vol. 1, p. 336.)

Lines 7 and 8: Literally, "and the pink body of pines/is naked in the sunset hour."

Index of Poem Titles and First Lines

JANE KENYON was born in Ann Arbor and graduated from the University of Michigan. She published four collections of poetry during her lifetime—*From Room to Room* (Alice James Books, 1978), *The Boat of Quiet Hours* (Graywolf Press, 1986), *Let Evening Come* (Graywolf Press, 1990), and *Constance* (Graywolf Press, 1993)—and a volume of translations, *Twenty Poems of Anna Akhmatova* (Eighties Press/Ally Press, 1985). She is the author of a posthumous collection: *Otherwise: New & Selected Poems* (Graywolf Press, 1996). *A Hundred White Daffodils* (Graywolf Press, 1999) collects Kenyon's essays, interviews, newspaper columns, and other work. She lived with her husband, Donald Hall, in Wilmot, New Hampshire, until her death in 1995.

This book is made possible through a partnership with the College of Saint Benedict, and honors the legacy of S. Mariella Gable, a distinguished teacher at the College.

Previous titles in the series include:

Loverboy by Victoria Redel
The House on Eccles Road by Judith Kitchen
One Vacant Chair by Joe Coomer
The Weatherman by Clint McCown

The text of *Collected Poems, Jane Kenyon* has been set in Adobe Garamond Pro, a typeface drawn by Robert Slimbach and based on type cut by Claude Garamond in the sixteenth century. Book design by Wendy Holdman. Composition at Prism Publishing Center. Manufactured by Maple Vail Book Manufacturing on acid-free paper.